"A Family's Quest For Rhythm is amazing. I want everyone to read this book because it puts into words the things that are impossible to put into words and explains things that are impossible to explain."

Mary Skorupa

Executive Director, Children's Mental Health Coalition of WNY, Inc. A Chapter of Families Together in NYS

"Parents of children who don't respond to textbook parenting techniques will find company, inspiration, and practical advice. This compelling story, framed in humor and compassion, is a must-read for parents of children with challenging behaviors and the professionals who work with them."

Dr. Helene Walisever

Clinical psychologist & author

"This book will be helpful for families struggling to understand and cope with challenging symptoms; it provides practical tips on what to do (and what not to do), what is often helpful (and what may instead be hurtful), and the different ways the affected individual and family are impacted."

Cathy L. Budman, M.D.

Movement Disorders Program, Hofstra University School of Medicine

"This remarkable memoir deals with the rages [and] other symptoms entailed in the complexities of Tourette syndrome…the issues, the hardships and the triumphs, with great sensitivity and insight. I recommend this book to any family struggling with similar problems, or to teachers, counselors or doctors who are involved with children with these complex disorders."

Dr. Ruth Dowling Bruun

Psychiatrist & author

"[This book] provides insight to parenting a child with challenging behaviors that can be a valuable addition to any professional working with children and families. I will be recommending this as a must-read to teachers who have students with challenging behaviors in their classes."

Dr. Ellen Contopidis, Ph.D.

Associate Professor of Inclusive Childhood Education, Nazareth College

A Family's Quest for Rhythm

Living with Tourette, ADD, OCD and Challenging Behaviors

Kathy Giordano

Matt Giordano

Front cover photograph by Paula Jones
Back cover photograph by John Cullen (used with permission
from John Cullen and the Tourette Syndrome Foundation of
Canada and @RANDOM)
Cover design and layout by Jennifer Rowe Creative Services

ISBN 978-1-105-97848-7

DEDICATION

To Tony, Erika, Jeff, Matthew, Jeannie and Dan, who not only are participants on this journey of ours, but allow us to share our family's difficult stories so that other families might benefit.
- Kathy Giordano

To everyone I mentioned and didn't mention in this book who has been part of my life's journey.
- Matt Giordano

Contents

DISCLAIMER 1

AUTHORS' NOTE..3

1   "YOUR FAMILY IS SO INTERESTING!"........................7

2   YOUR CHILD'S DIAGNOSIS IS… 11

3   THE LAST TOUCH, LAST WORD, LAST HURT..............19

4   NEUROLOGICAL RAGE 25

5   WHAT CAN WE DO DURING A RAGE EPISODE?...........35

6   RESIDENTIAL PLACEMENT 41

7   FOSTER PLACEMENT 55

8   THE IMPORTANCE OF BALANCE..........................63

9   THE IMPORTANCE OF BALANCE FOR PARENTS 73

10   DESPERATE TO FIND THE ANSWER 79

11   HOPE—THE OTHER FOUR LETTER WORD 93

12   A QUEST FOR COMPANIONS ON THE JOURNEY 101

13   THE "SEVERE SUPPORT GROUP"..........................109

14   EFFECT ON OUR FAMILY 113

15   TEACHERS ON OUR TEAM...............................123

16   MANAGING SYMPTOMS AND LEARNING
     LIFE STRATEGIES.......................................143

17   WHEN IT'S OVER, IT'S DONE—FOR THEM..............151

18   TONY'S THOUGHTS.....................................155

19   HELLO THERE! MY NAME IS MATT.....................163

20   VALUABLE LIFE LESSONS..............................177

21   REFLECTIONS OF A PROUD MOM........................187

FINAL THOUGHTS 193

RESOURCES 195

ABOUT THE AUTHORS 197

DISCLAIMER

This book is meant to be motivational for our readers. It is sold with the understanding that the authors and publisher are not qualified or intending to render any type of medical, psychological, legal, or any other kind of professional advice. This book is not meant to be used, nor should it be used, to diagnose or treat any medical condition. For diagnosis or treatment of any medical problem, consult your own physician.

The content of this book is the sole expression and opinion of its authors, and not necessarily that of the publisher, The Advocacy Center or the Tourette Syndrome Association, Inc. Neither the publisher nor the individual authors shall be liable for any physical, psychological, emotional, financial, or commercial damages, including, but not limited to, special, incidental, consequential or other damages. References are provided for informational purposes. Readers should be aware that the websites listed in this book may change. Our views and rights are the same: You are responsible for your own choices, actions, and results.

Authors' Note
Conversation We Hope Helps Others

We are long past the 'bad years'; past the years of holes in the walls, broken windows, threats and out-of-control behaviors. Past the years of our son asking why God made him this way and if we would be happier if he hadn't been born.

We are grateful that we have three incredibly wonderful adult children, are still married and still relatively sane. An important reason for all of this is our "conversations" with parents who lived similar lives. They validated that we weren't alone, it wasn't our fault, or our child's fault. They gave us the strength to continue. Additional credit goes to the professionals who didn't judge or blame us.

We know, however, that there are still parents of children with challenging behaviors who are wrongfully blamed, just as we were. We know there are parents who feel isolated, frustrated and helpless as their child becomes more depressed and angry while symptoms increase. We hope that by reading this you will find some reassurance that having a child with symptoms that include challenging behavior is not your child's fault, and it's not your fault.

Our journey began over 27 years ago. Knowledge and acceptance of disorders with challenging behaviors have changed since then. Strategies that focus on positive interventions are finally replacing the belief that punishment and rewards are always the most effective way to deal with challenging behaviors.

Awareness regarding how the brain functions and the impact of chemical imbalances has come a long way. Unfortunately, there continue to be some people who are not well-informed and cling to the notion that children with challenging behaviors must be punished.

As our family looks back, we are not filled with anger or regrets. Instead we recognize and appreciate the compassion, generosity, knowledge, support and kindness of those who helped along the way. There are an amazing number of people who were involved in our journey. I have ended chapters with stories about some of them. I am hopeful that these stories illustrate the importance of people helping families with similar difficulties and encourage parents to recognize the importance of accepting assistance from people who can provide valuable supports.

I am often asked how Matt and I can share our story during presentations, and now in this book. I see Matt as being much braver than I for his openness and honesty. It helps that audiences are immediately captivated by his charm, his talent and his humor, recognizing that his story is one of an incredible person who has survived a difficult childhood.

It would be much easier to write about the good times. I could share Matthew's 'creative' attempts at making me breakfast in bed, or the weekly Saturday morning drives to his drum lessons as he air-drummed to a recording of "Jesus Christ Superstar" with so much drama and flair that we both laughed. There were many happy and tender times—holding my hand when he sensed that I was sad, our walks in the woods, the loving and often humorous messages that he still leaves on my voice mail, and so much more.

Many people have known Matt since he was young and are very aware that he experienced extremely challenging childhood symptoms and miraculously overcame them. But for those of you who haven't had the pleasure of meeting him, it's important that you know that he has always been the best son a mother could hope for.

We are able to share these difficult stories because neurological differences are not something to be ashamed of, just as no one should be ashamed of *any* medical diagnosis. There were times when all of us were frustrated by symptoms, but I have always been proud of my son and constantly reinforced that he should always be proud of who he is as well.

Primarily, we share our stories because our hope is that our 'conversation' will provide some insight and reassurance that will assist you on *your* family's journey.

Okay, let's begin the conversation.

- 1 -

"YOUR FAMILY IS SO INTERESTING!"

We lived fairly uninteresting lives for years. Tony and I married in 1973 and by 1982 we had three children; a girl and two boys, two dogs and a cat.

We lived in the country, on a dirt road in a log house that we helped build. Since this was back in the 1970s, the "town people" called the few young families who lived on our hill the "Hippie Hill People." Okay, so we were somewhat interesting!

Our first two children had minor issues, typical of many young children. Erika had some attention deficits and obsessive/compulsive tendencies. Jeff stuttered as a little boy and had seizures, which were brought on by fevers. Both the stuttering and seizures disappeared when he was seven.

Maybe we weren't the typical all-American family, but no one described our lives as "interesting." "Interesting" didn't happen until after our youngest son, Matthew, was five and diagnosed with Tourette syndrome, attention deficit disorder, obsessive compulsive disorder, oppositional defiant disorder, anxiety, neurological rage and symptoms that became severe and dangerous.

For years, professionals who worked with us would almost always say at one time or another, "Your family is so interesting." They said it as if it were a grand compliment. I'm certain they didn't realize how this raised the hairs on the back of my neck. Back then, it made me feel as if my family was a specimen to be studied. There were times when I longed for boring. I thought boring would be nice. But that was not to be our lot in life.

We were seen as interesting because people quickly recognized that Matthew's challenging behaviors were in stark contrast to who he was as a person. Additionally, they saw that we were loving parents. Our family didn't fit any category that the professionals had learned about. We weren't similar to other families they had worked with who had major behavior issues in their homes. Thus, we were "interesting."

About the same time that people began to find us "interesting," some of them were telling me that I should write about our experience. I was told that it would help other families to know that they were not alone.

During those bad years, I didn't see the sense in writing about my family living this hell. And to be totally honest, I was just too tired and incapable of anything more than putting one foot in front of the other in an attempt at getting through each day. When our lives began to be less traumatic, I felt that I couldn't write our story until I could end with something more than "interesting." I wanted to have a happy last chapter. Not syrupy or saccharine happy—but one with a positive outcome. I can now do that! If you'd like to see why that's true, either before or during your reading of this book, read the last chapter "Reflections of A Proud Mom."

Matthew's birth was actually *slightly* interesting, but as I speak to other parents, it wasn't all that unusual for children with similar difficulties. He was our third child, so we assumed we knew what we were doing—always a dangerous supposition.

Two months before my due date, I woke up thinking that I was having Braxton-Hicks contractions. By the next afternoon, while Tony was at work, there was no doubt about whether I was or wasn't in labor—I *was*! I called one of my neighbors, told her what was going on and asked if I could borrow her car to drive to the hospital. Within minutes, all of my neighbors were in my front yard! They agreed unanimously that I should go to the hospital, but I shouldn't drive myself. It was decided that Lynn should drive because she had helped numerous horses and cows give birth and would know what to do if we didn't make it to the hospital in time. Thank goodness, we *did* make it on time!

As it turned out, I was in premature labor and ended up staying at the hospital on total bed rest for the next six weeks. My labor never stopped the entire time. Since the baby's lungs weren't developed yet, the doctors gave me medication which reduced the intensity of the contractions. After a month, tests indicated that it was finally safe to deliver the baby, so they discontinued medication and sent me home. And wouldn't you know, the contractions stopped completely for the first time in over six weeks! Ahhhh, the beginning of Matthew doing things on *his* time frame and in *his* way.

After a week without contractions, my water broke suddenly at 5 a.m. Tony needed a haircut for an important meeting that was coming up, so I gave him the fastest hair cut in history, woke up Erika and Jeff, and raced to the hospital. Thankfully, it was a Saturday morning and there were few other cars on the road to slow us down. Matthew was born within 45 minutes of our arriving at the hospital.

He was beautiful and healthy! There was no reason to believe or even suspect that this perfect little baby would put an end to our ordinary and uninteresting lives. Nothing would have led me to suspect that in 10 years we would attend a concert at the prestigious Eastman Theater to see our son perform. Nor were there any hints that in eight years we would be sitting in the waiting area for an appointment with the director of a children's psychiatric center.

I never could have imagined that this healthy, curious and happy baby would eventually be the impetus for my dedicating my life to educating and supporting people regarding neuro-behavior disorders—and eventually to writing about our journey as a family.

DAWN

Almost 16 years ago, when I began working as an advocate/service coordinator for children with disabilities, I met Dawn. After we had completed the obligatory paperwork, her six-year-old son came in from playing. Dawn introduced me as his new service coordinator. I extended my hand with the intention of beginning a relationship based on respect. He looked at my hand and his eyes lit up. It was only when he put his hand in mine that I understood why. He had been outside catching frogs and his hand was slimy with mud and other "things" that I preferred not to consider.

The look in his eyes and smile expressed his joy at having the opportunity to play a trick on this strange adult person. I laughed, wiped my hand on his already very dirty shirt—and was impressed.

I so love the glint in the eye, the quick wit and charming personalities that many children with these "disorders" possess. Getting a child through school and into adulthood without destroying that spirit is what supporting children is all about.

Dawn and her son represent all of the parents and children I have worked with over the years and from whom I have learned so much. Thank you! I would not have been able to write this without you. Thank you for allowing me to be involved in your lives and to learn so much from your experiences, your strategies and your successes.

- 2 -

YOUR CHILD'S DIAGNOSIS IS...

I first started noticing that some of Matthew's behaviors were unusual when he was two. He was constantly rubbing his nose and immediately touching his cheek. He would occasionally make unusual noises or repeat a sound or word over and over. I described this to his pediatrician. He told me my youngest son was just an active little boy. He added that he may be one of those kids who would experience numerous minor mishaps; however, there was nothing to worry about. So I didn't worry about it.

The behaviors became more bizarre, more frequent and more intense. I brought him back to the same doctor who again explained that some boys are calmer than others (like my first son, Jeff) and once again told me that some children are more active. This didn't explain for me why Matthew was constantly licking his fingers, touching his toes and then touching his right eyeball. It didn't help me understand why he screamed, hit and punched me if I attempted to stop him from behaviors that were destructive or harmful to him. But the doctor continued to insist that there was nothing wrong and that I was worrying too much.

When Matthew began Kindergarten, the behaviors at home increased tenfold. One spring day, I was working out in the yard when the school bus stopped at the end of our driveway. As soon as Matthew walked off the bus, I heard a loud squealing followed by high-pitched screeches. I followed him into the house where he immediately laid on the floor and began jerking so violently that his body lifted off the flooring. Since I had experienced seizures with my older son, I knew that was not what was occurring.

After a few minutes of this, he went to the basement. He lay on the linoleum floor, and for the next two hours, spun on his back in a circle saying, "God damn-it" over and over. He said it in a loud and high-pitched voice, which prior to this I would have thought was humanly impossible. Every few minutes he would stop to beg me for help. When I attempted to hold him in my arms or even offer a suggestion, he would hit me and scream for me to "BE QUIET!" Clearly he hated what he was doing, but was somehow compelled to do it and my attempts to help only infuriated him.

I certainly didn't know how to help him or what was happening to my son. There had been other behaviors that we had noticed and thought were odd but lots of little kids do strange things that they outgrow...this, however, was way outside of the norm.

Up until then, I had succeeded in ignoring my parental gut feelings that were constantly reminding me that something was majorly not right. The next day, I called the pediatrician's office to ask if I could make an appointment to speak with the doctor without my son present. The receptionist forwarded my call to the nurse. I explained that my son was demonstrating very strange behaviors and I needed to meet with the doctor in private to discuss them. The nurse told me that I would have to make an appointment for my son to have a physical, after which I could then speak with the doctor. I explained that he had recently had a physical and that because my son's behaviors were getting more bizarre, I needed to discuss this without my son being present.

I read to her the following list:
- *Tongue Itches—he rubs it against his front teeth until it bleeds & blisters*
- *Spits on his sleeve*
- *Makes noises over and over*

- When he has had sugar or hasn't had any food for a while, he does jerking motions. Sometimes they are slight, sometimes extreme
- Complains that people are breathing in his mouth if they are near him
- Temper—small things annoy him terribly—example, my daughter sniffing or my husband clearing his throat

The pediatrician's nurse told me in most instances, behaviors like this were an attempt to gain attention. ATTENTION! It seemed to me a really extraordinary and bizarre way to get attention.

She continued to insist that I couldn't meet with the doctor without my son present because it was against their policy. I thought what I was requesting was reasonable. This doctor knew all my children and was the only pediatrician who had seen Matthew since his birth. Needless to say, I was confused and irritated. I didn't know it at the time, but this would be the first of many instances when I would be told that what I was requesting was not *policy*. I was expected to quietly accept this—even though what I was asking made perfect sense, at least to me. I believed their policy could be overlooked under these circumstances.

Since we lived in a rural area, there were only two pediatricians within a 50 mile radius. As soon as I hung up with this nurse, I dragged out the phone book and called the other pediatrician. I repeated my request for a private discussion with the doctor regarding my son's unusual behaviors.

The receptionist asked if we were regular patients. I told her that we weren't, but I was very concerned regarding my son's behaviors and wanted to speak to the doctor about them. She put me on hold and when she returned, I was given an appointment later that day.

Matthew came with me because I couldn't find a babysitter. He sat in the outer office as I spoke to Dr. Joan Flender for the first time. We discussed my list of concerns. After we had talked, she asked if by any chance my son were with me. She spent a few minutes talking with Matthew about school and what he liked to do for fun. She sent him back to the waiting room and told me that she thought she knew what his diagnosis was. She assured me that it was not life threatening and should not cause us considerable concern. But, she asked if my husband and I could meet with her that evening to discuss it.

When I returned to her office with my husband, it was the first time we heard the words "Tourette syndrome." She explained that she had done her residency with a pediatric neurologist and strongly suspected this diagnosis because of the repetitive behaviors I had described and others that she had witnessed. She drew two lines on both ends of the paper that covered the table, representing a scale from mild to severe, and explained that people have varying levels of symptoms. She added that our son's symptoms were very mild, pointing to a spot closest to the "mild" end of the table. She assured us that most likely his symptoms would remain at that level. (Okay, so she miscalculated this a tad!)

Dr. Flender said that if we were in agreement, she would make an appointment for Matthew with Dr. Sarah Roddy, the pediatric neurologist with whom she had interned and whose practice was in a nearby city. We agreed. She asked me to call her office the next day and her receptionist would tell me the time for his appointment, adding that she would do what she could to get it as quickly as possible.

On the way home, my husband said he didn't understand why it was necessary to see another doctor because we now had a diagnosis. Why did we need to see another doctor who would tell us the same thing? I wasn't sure either, but once again, I listened to my parent gut feeling and it seemed to me to be a good idea.

Even with Dr. Flender's influence, the appointment couldn't be scheduled for at least two more months. During that time, symptoms escalated and became increasingly dangerous. Matthew hated what was happening to him. My little five year old cried himself to sleep many nights after asking me over and over why God hated him and would we be better off if he were dead?

The day for the appointment finally arrived. I signed in at the reception desk and we waited to be called. After what seemed like a long time, a nurse called my name. I began to stand up but she walked over to where we were sitting. She told me that there must be some mistake; our appointment wasn't until next month. For the first time, I totally understood the concept of having the rug pulled out from under me. I had been looking forward to this day with increasing desperation as things had become more and more violent at home. I was hopeful that since there was a diagnosis, coupled with the fact that we were seeing a doctor who specialized in this disorder, that there would be a cure. Was I really hearing her correctly? Was she saying that we had to somehow survive an additional month?

I looked up with tears in my eyes, something I rarely experience, and said to her, "I'm afraid if we have to wait that long, someone will be dead by then."

I didn't say it as a ploy to see the doctor—I was serious and terrified. She must have recognized my desperation because she disappeared into the back and when she returned, said that Dr. Roddy would see us.

After putting Matthew through some neurological testing that we would become used to every time we had an appointment with her, she agreed with the diagnosis. She wrote a prescription and asked us to set up a return appointment for three months. I was happy. We had a diagnosis and medication that I was convinced would return my son to his loving, kind self.

Unfortunately, it didn't.

But at least we had the correct diagnosis. I have known many families who struggled getting a diagnosis for years. Parents who know that something is going on, but all too often are treated as if they are exaggerating the symptoms. The majority of doctors in the 1980s weren't knowledgeable regarding the unusual and inconsistent symptoms of many neuro-behavioral disorders. This often resulted in a long delay, or worse, a wrong diagnosis with wrong medications. I have seen the wasted years, the frustration, the pain, and the years of punishment instead of support. I have seen the damage done to a marriage, a family and a child because of the blame and shame approach—all because of a misdiagnosis resulting in a miscalculation of the child's *needs.*

I have seen too many children punished for symptoms they can't control, inappropriate interventions and parents who are blamed and made to feel guilty. Delays or inaccurate diagnoses result in teachers, family members and friends who believe the child is purposefully misbehaving. Worst, the child also believes that he or she is bad.

I was, not surprisingly, torn by this diagnosis. On one hand, I had never heard of it and anything that required an appointment to a pediatric neurologist's office must be pretty serious. On the other hand, the diagnosis meant that my son's behavior was not his fault or mine. Instead of being depressed that my son *had* a diagnosis, I actually had a sense of relief. If there was a medical name, there must be a medication and a cure! Plus, it wasn't anyone's fault!

Many people say that when they get a diagnosis of this magnitude, they grieve the loss of their dream for the child. I don't remember that occurring for me. I didn't have a clue what Tourette syndrome was or what it meant for us, but I knew we would get through it.

As it turned out, I'm grateful to the first pediatrician's nurse. Because of a strict adherence to their policy, we were fortunate to receive treatment from Dr. Flender, who recognized Tourette syndrome immediately. To say this was unusual back in the late 1980s is putting it mildly. Additionally, she referred us to a neurologist instead of a psychiatrist, as most pediatricians would have done, and which I suspect would not have resulted in as positive an outcome.

I'm still not sure exactly what made me call Dr. Flender's office when I was not able to speak privately with my children's regular pediatrician. To write that I am profoundly grateful that I followed my parental instincts to find another doctor may be the biggest understatement of this entire book. When Matthew was a toddler, I never expected that I would someday be looking for a diagnosis for my son. But, life often has different plans for us than what we expect. By the time a doctor told me that she thought she knew the diagnosis for him, it was actually a relief.

With a diagnosis, we had something to hold onto; there was actually a *reason* for what was happening to our bright and delightful little boy; he had a "syndrome." We didn't know it at the time, but we had begun our journey—a journey that would have a major impact not only on Matthew's life, but also on our entire family, our friends, the community and my life's work.

DR. JOAN FLENDER

How can we possibly thank you enough?! I only wish that all doctors were as knowledgeable, dedicated and genuinely kind. Your office accepted a call from a desperate mother who was given an appointment the same day even though she had never been in your office before that day.

You spoke to me because that is what I needed and it was the right thing to do. You took time to speak to Matthew with curiosity rather than a preconceived notion. You gave me reassurance before I left as well as a follow-up meeting for that evening when your office was closed. We weren't even your regular patients!

You could have referred us to parenting classes or a professional who would have focused on determining which parent was at fault for a child who swore and was aggressive primarily only in his home. You could have encouraged us to use punishment in our attempts at controlling the "difficult behaviors." The incredible fact is—you didn't.

Because you believed us, you and Dr. Roddy were the foundation upon which my son's life has been built. Instead of shame, blame, punishment and anger, you set the stage for us to develop strategies and techniques to assist him in managing his symptoms in a way that would lead him to a life of independence and success.

Just as the foundation of a house is critical to its stability, I am certain that you and Dr. Roddy were the major reason for the continued stability of our marriage, our children's lives and our family. Neither of you ever wavered in your support of our son, or of us as good parents who struggled with these complex and highly misunderstood disorders. Thank you for believing in us, for not making assumptions, for providing the correct diagnoses so that correct interventions and supports could be provided; and for being an incredible doctor to my son for over 15 years.

If any of the readers are ever at Noyes Hospital in Dansville, NY, check out the wall that has pictures of participating physicians. You'll see Dr. Flender's immediately. She's the one whose lab coat has pictures of cartoon characters!

- 3 -

THE LAST TOUCH, LAST WORD, LAST HURT

Even though we had a diagnosis, we weren't prepared for the peculiar and difficult-to-explain nature of the violent/aggressive symptoms. Primarily, they were only present at home. If they occurred away from home, they were directed only toward family members. There were all sorts of speculations as to why this occurred:

- The child feels safe at home to express any and all symptoms
- The child knows that the parents will love them no matter what
- The child suppresses symptoms all day, every day and the exhaustion, frustration and difficulty of this leads to an explosion at home
- The home is not as structured as the school or residential settings
- Extreme anger at his parents for not being able to make him better
- Chemical changes of all mammals occur when they are both away from and when they are in 'their nest'
- And, of course, bad parenting

Matthew, at the age of seven, gave me another explanation. I had asked him why he hurts Mommy and Daddy. He compared it to his need to get the last touch. Just as he *needed* to get the last touch, he *needed* to get the last word. Most horrible, however, was that if the situation was exceptionally unpleasant for him, he *needed* to get the last hurt.

So, if a person he loved was being hurt, this made him feel bad. Since that person, in effect, had been the reason that he felt bad, he needed to hurt that person again to get the last hurt.

It's much easier to understand a person's compulsive need to 'even up' pencils on a desk, toys, silverware or belongings on the dresser. I know people who must touch something with their left hand if they have touched it first with their right hand. Some have an overwhelming need when they touch something white to touch something black. It's referred to as *'evening up.'*

As a young child, Matthew had a *need* for 'evening up' difficult emotions. Not in a controlled, thoughtful way, but as a compulsive need that didn't make any more sense than if he had needed to 'even up' objects. If someone made him angry, he had an overwhelming need to do something that would make that person angry. If someone he loved hurt his feelings, he needed to hurt that person. Unfortunately, when he did 'even up' by hurting that person, he would again be hurt emotionally which re-ignited his need to once again get the last hurt.

As I'm sure it's not difficult to imagine, this symptom caused numerous episodes in which Matthew was out-of-control in his attempts to satisfy the compulsion while members of the family would attempt to protect themselves in various ways.

I remember a middle school boy who had to get the last touch. Five of his classmates discovered this and at the end of the day, they would all touch him at the same time and then run to different busses. The boy's frustration at not being able to complete his *need* to get the last touch nearly resulted in his breakdown.

Similarly, Matthew was often frustrated and took out his anger by doing physical damage. As a result, our house had many broken windows and holes or dents in all of the interior walls. Additionally, anything that was considered to be of value to anyone of us had to be hidden so that it wouldn't be damaged. An advantage of living in a log home was that the exterior walls remained undamaged. We discontinued using drinking glasses and went to heavy-duty mugs that could withstand being bounced off the floor. Kitchen chairs were broken, glued, broken and re-glued; eventually we ended up using metal folding chairs.

We had at least three different kinds of punching bags. None of them helped. We drew a bull's-eye on the side of our woodshed for him to throw balls at which made a loud noise. This was sometimes helpful for him. I have since heard of a mother who would buy cheap dishes at garage sales. There was a room built in their basement where their child, who had a similar need to 'even up,' could go to, put on safety gear, then throw and break dishes into a deep box.

Looking back at this, I know we tried to find ways for him to complete his *need*, but now I wish I had been more creative with strategies. Maybe we could have thought of some way for him to get the last hurt that would have satisfied his compulsion while also being safe. But, to be totally honest with you, as I write that sentence it feels very familiar to how I felt so long ago during my constant struggle to find an answer that would help my son. Maybe that never goes away.

Fortunately no one ever required a trip to the emergency room. But emotionally it was hard on all of us. Jeff would usually go for a bike ride, a walk, go to his room or climb up onto the roof of our woodshed until things calmed down.
Erika had Diane's house.

EDIE & RAY PHILIPSON

Erika met Edie and Ray's daughter, Diane, in nursery school at the age of four. They remain close friends today, 32 years later. Ray and Edie, are some of our closest friends.

During the difficult years, Edie and Ray never asked questions; they simply opened their hearts and their home to Erika. There were times when I just needed to find safe places for my other children. Places where the environment 'made sense' and wasn't filled with violence, yelling, swearing, screaming and chaos. I had a difficult time explaining this to others, but Edie understood in a way for which I will forever be grateful.

I don't know how she knew; maybe she could hear it in my voice. There were countless times I called on the phone and when Edie heard it was me she asked, without any hesitation, if Erika wanted to come over to play. The amazing thing is, I didn't need to ask—she knew and offered with no need of any explanation or reason.

So many times people would make subtle comments indicating they questioned how we were parenting our children. Never, not even once, did I ever feel any judgment from them. Never did they ask why we couldn't control the situation and be better parents. Never did they question our ability to provide a safe home and a nurturing environment for our daughter.

Edie and Ray drove their family to Florida every year and every year they took Erika with them. Family vacations were something we couldn't provide for our children, but for Erika, Ray and Edie could…and they did.

One year, after Erika had gone on vacation with them for the umpteenth time, Ray joked that they should be able to include Erika on their income tax as a deduction. It was true—they should have. I could not afford to give them the money to cover Erika's expenses on these vacations. Due to all the expenses for medications, numerous therapists and doctors, we barely made ends meet. Edie and Ray never asked for any money. I would try to do what I could to repay them, but of course I never could and never will. They are dear, dear friends who helped us more than they could possibly know.

They provided a second family for Erika; an intact 'normal' family. I knew that she was safe there and that they loved her as if she was their daughter. In their home, Edie and Ray have a long hallway between their kitchen and living room. Edie filled the wall with photos of their children at different ages. There on the wall is a picture of Erika. Not a photo of her with any of their other children—just Erika! A picture of the little girl that was part of their family. What a tremendous blessing they have been not only for Erika but for our entire family. Thanks, guys!

- 4 -

NEUROLOGICAL RAGE

Here's how Matt describes his feelings of rage in his chapter:

> When I was a kid having such extreme rage episodes, it
> was a scary thing for everyone, including me. I
> remember that I didn't have control of these rage
> episodes any more than I had control over my tics or
> OCD episodes. I just couldn't stop myself. When the
> rage finally calmed down, I felt like the worst person on
> the planet. I couldn't believe that I treated the people I
> loved the most in such a terrible way. I always felt
> responsible, even though I wasn't. Intellectually, I knew
> it was the Tourette's, but the guilt was still
> overwhelming. After I had lost control and hurt the ones
> I loved, it wasn't as if I looked at myself in the mirror
> and thought, 'It's the Tourette's fault. No big deal.' I
> always believed that it was my fault. I blamed myself
> even though I knew it was my symptoms' fault and I had
> no control over any of these behaviors. It didn't matter
> though. I was the one who hurt the people I love, and I
> was the one who always felt so terrible about it.

As Matthew's mother and someone who works with
educators and parents, I have heard people describe neurological
rage in a variety of ways. Some people describe it as being
similar to a seizure in the section of the brain responsible for
emotions; others as faulty mental brakes. I recently heard a
description that painted a picture of water pipes that have a

malfunctioning relief valve and as the temperature rises and steam develops, the pipes burst.

One could also compare the neurological system to the digestive system when it has taken in more than it can hold, resulting in vomiting. All of these descriptions share the accurate concept that rage episodes are not purposeful and definitely not your typical, run-of-the mill temper tantrums.

The rage we lived with was unlike anything I had ever known was possible. It would erupt like a volcano—fast, violent, without warning, and beyond my ability to control on any level. As a parent I felt as helpless as if my child was in the midst of a full blown seizure. I always had the desire to hug Matthew thinking that would make it "all better," the rage would end and *my son*, who was present five minutes ago, would be able to return. Not only was that a ridiculous concept, it would have been physically impossible for me to hold him during a rage.

Rage increased his strength considerably and somehow gave him the stamina to continue for hours. Only people who have witnessed one can have a true concept of the inconceivable intensity that was maintained for two, three and even four hours. It's almost impossible to comprehend that any child could do this, but it's even more difficult to imagine that a child as kind and gentle as Matthew could be held hostage by that level of anger and violence for such an extraordinary length of time.

We all know what anger looks like and even sometimes what initiates it. There are many levels of being angry—flying off the handle, ticked off, irritated, mad, angry, very angry, extremely angry, totally losing it...yet none of these come close to describing neurological rage.

Rage! Unrelenting, unreachable, inextinguishable *rage!* No amount of threats, spankings, punishment, removing privileges or taking away prized possessions would either prevent one from occurring or extinguish one. We removed every toy from his room—it didn't matter at all. We had charts offering amazing rewards—not only did this have no impact what-so-ever, but often the charts would end up in a crumpled mass thrown across the room. It took us *way* too long to finally realize that rewards and punishments work *only* if the child has control over the behavior. We eventually learned that they don't work in the slightest when behaviors are a result of a chemical imbalance that impacts the brain in a manner which diminishes the child's ability to inhibit behaviors.

"Causing" the rage could be anything from saying the word no, getting in the way of completing a compulsion, breathing "wrong," saying something "wrong" or for reasons that we never were able to determine, understand or predict.

Matthew kicked holes in his bedroom wall as high as his feet or fists could reach until very little wall was left. I tried hanging some of the beautiful artwork he had created on his walls, knowing how much he prized them hoping that would stop the destruction. It made no difference. Because he repeatedly broke his bedroom windows on the second floor, we were concerned about him falling out. We moved him to the downstairs bedroom. This didn't stop him from breaking windows, but it did make it a little safer if he should happen to fall out or even climb out.

We eventually had to cover the windows with the same type of Plexiglas that is used behind hockey nets. My husband assured me that this would definitely work! At the age of seven, however, Matthew managed to break even these. We covered the windows in his room with plywood. We found that we needed to place nails every inch so he wouldn't be able to get his fingers under the board and rip it off. Other windows in the house were occasionally broken either during a rage or because he *needed* to throw his shoe as hard as he could at the window *frame*. Since his aim was less than precise, the shoe sometimes hit and broke the glass instead.

Attempts at stopping rage most often only increased the length and intensity of the episode. If we tried to hold him, he would do anything and everything to get away. Sometimes we had no choice and we had to lock him in his room for his and others' safety. I suspect this is illegal, so I hope that the statutes of limitations on such things are long past.

Driving anywhere in the car was a nightmare. It may have been due to being confined in such a small space, breathing people's "germs," or the bumping as we drove on dirt roads near our house. Maybe it was because he knew that his symptoms were unpredictable which led to fear of what lie ahead, which increased his anxiety and resulted in increased level of symptoms. Who knows? But for safety, we rarely drove anywhere unless Tony or I could ride in the backseat next to Matthew.

People would ask us, "Why don't you make him stop?" or "Why do you let him get away with this?" or "You need to give him a good spanking or a good talking to." Frankly, I've always wondered why we adults use the word "good" in those last phrases—I seem to remember as a child seeing nothing "good" about either.

"Just make him behave!" Parents of a child with this type of rage understand when I say, we *couldn't* make him behave and punishments for rage never worked. One or our counselors, JoAnn, once said to me that parents are able to punish a child only as much as that child will allow him or herself to be punished. At first, I thought this was one of the most bizarre things I had ever heard. But when I thought about it, it made a great deal of sense—for us at least. If I told my older children to go to their room, they may have complained, they may have slammed the door—but they would still go to their rooms. Unlike this, any attempts at punishing Matthew only escalated his rage.

The amazing thing is that even as I write that, it sounds ridiculous to me! What do you mean, *he wouldn't* accept punishment—*Just Punish Him*! Okay, how? We could have beaten him and, sadly, there were times we came very close to being *too* physical toward him; but we couldn't make him "go" to his room. We had to carry him kicking and screaming. And even though we consistently did this—it didn't change anything. His rage would continue at full strength for hours until he fell asleep from pure exhaustion. It didn't teach him a lesson or decrease the likelihood that it would not happen later that same day or the next day, or the day after that. Keep punishing him, you say? We DID! It didn't help!

People insisted that consistently punishing him would eventually help! It would demonstrate that we were in charge! At some point, he would behave better because he didn't want to be punished again! My answer to these statements is: No, it didn't, No, it didn't, and No, it didn't! *Nothing* made a difference.

Actually that's not entirely true. Some things *did* make a difference, but they weren't positive in nature. If we yelled, threatened, punished, spanked, etc. it would *increase* his rage. Which, when I think about it now, makes sense. Matthew's brain chemistry never allowed him to have just a *little* bit of anger, or a *little* bit of fear. For some children with challenging behaviors, the part of the brain that is responsible for inhibiting physical, verbal and emotional responses may malfunction. For some, it malfunctions a little and for others it malfunctions in a big way. It's similar to the "dimmer switch" in your brain not working consistently. Many times it seemed that the brain's anger was either fully off or fully on and nothing in between.

One day I noticed that Matthew's eyes during these rage episodes looked like a trapped animal fighting for his life. It suddenly made some sense to me. Since we humans are mammals, if my son was feeling threatened and cornered, having an adult acting aggressively toward him would not translate to calming him or de-escalating the situation. With his brain already in a state of fear, what did we expect to happen when we yelled, spanked, made threats, screamed and overall looked more threatening? It seems to make sense that his survival instinct of fighting back would be increased, not decreased. Additionally, it makes sense that his adrenaline would spike. The fight or flight mode that nature has provided us for self-survival, combined with his increased adrenaline, made situations very difficult and dangerous. As I got louder and more threatening, it was similar to throwing gasoline on an already blazing inferno.

Try to visualize what it must be like to be a child whose parent, the person you depend upon to ultimately know what to do and to keep you safe, yells and/or threatens you when your world is already spinning out of control. I suspect that you would see this person as *also* being out of control. How must this feel as a child? Certainly not *calming*.

I believe it is possible that part of the reason for his rage was Matthew being totally overwhelmed by an environment that was not conducive to his complex symptoms. This resulted in huge anxiety and impacted his neuro-chemical balance. Therefore, it wasn't difficult for me to consider that it was the chemical imbalances that were the reason for the intensity and the duration of the rage, not my son.

A favorite quote of mine is one by Joseph Chilton Pearce: "Anxiety is always the enemy of intelligence. The minute anxiety arises, intelligence closes to search for anything that relieves the anxiety." When anxiety spikes, the brain searches for anything to reduce the all-consuming anxiety. Toss in increased adrenaline and we may have the reason for rage. Matthew's needs drove him to a place that the majority of us only experience once or twice in a lifetime. We may experience this level of fear, anxiety and increased adrenaline after a car accident or a horrific event. Try to think of times when you were taken over by extreme anger and/or fear, which led to your doing and saying things that you would typically never do or say. Now imagine this occurring every day of your life and your parents not only don't make it go away, they yell and become frightening as well.

When I think back to those times, I feel deep sadness for Matthew and my other children. My sweet little boy who literally would not hurt a fly, unable to stop himself from breaking prized processions, destroying his own room and hurting people he loved. Well, actually, to be honest, I did often feel both sadness and anger back then and did things that I regret. One day I was walking upstairs and he threw a glass of grape juice in my face. I lost it! I chased him down and began slapping him over and over.

Fortunately Tony was nearby and pulled me off. I went outside, fell to my knees and cried. I was exhausted and frustrated with my inability to help my son. I was doing everything I could do to understand, but nothing was working. In fact, things were getting much worse. I knew instinctively that it wasn't my little boy who would purposefully experience rage. I tried to be patient, but there were many times I just plain failed.

Matthew apologized every single time. I wish that I could go back and apologize for those years when I responded by being bigger and louder to show him that I was the adult and I was in charge!

DONNA SPILLMAN

One day I answered the phone and a woman named Donna said that we had a mutual friend Marcy, who told her about our family. Donna was a school bus driver for children in special education programs. She told me that she would like to spend time with our son, which would provide "respite" for us. I had no idea what "respite" was. She explained that it was a time for Matthew to have fun while the rest of the family could do whatever we wanted. She suggested that she meet him and see if he would like to spend a Saturday every month going to the movies, sledding or other activities of his choice that he might enjoy.

No matter how tempting this sounded, I wasn't ready to turn my son over to someone I had never met. I told Donna that I would need to think it over and I would call her back. I spoke with Marcy who I had developed a friendship with while working together on the town's all-volunteer newspaper. She knew Matthew and the level of his symptoms as she had included him in many of their family gatherings. Marcy told me that she and Donna had known each other for years because they both were volunteer fire fighters for our town. She said that Donna was a woman who loved children, and was still somewhat of a kid herself. She had spoken with Donna about our family and told me if Matthew were her son, she would take Donna up on her offer.

Tony and I decided to let Donna spend half a day with Matthew so they could get to know each other and go from there.

We knew that he always did very well with people outside of the family and particularly when involved in activities that he enjoyed. I brought Matthew to Donna's house, gave her my phone number, talked for a bit and left. As I drove home, I suddenly was filled with the fear that we may have made a terrible mistake. I kept reminding myself that Marcy had assured us that Donna was a close and trusted friend of hers.

When Donna and Matthew returned home after their day out, he was happier than I had seen him in a long time. He was *really* happy. Donna called later and said that she had enjoyed the day as well and would like to make it a monthly event for her and Matthew to do something special together.

Donna occasionally took Matthew for an entire weekend so that Tony and I could drive to Toronto. Our rule was that after we were more than 50 miles away from home, neither of us could talk about any of our children. These weekends away were truly wonderful for our relationship. While walking around Toronto, stopping in at Jazz clubs, we were able to remember why we married each other. We actually *did* still love each other!

Donna and Matthew continued to meet for years. As a teenager, it was more difficult to 'hang out' and the visits became less frequent. One tradition that lasted throughout the years was to meet just prior to Halloween. Donna would bring him to a pumpkin patch and buy him the largest pumpkin they could find. I sometimes still find the largest pumpkin and enjoy those happy memories.

I will never be able to thank Donna enough for making Matthew feel special. They had exciting adventures one day a month, and Tony and I had a day as a couple or to spend with Erika and Jeff. Those Saturdays represented only 12 out of 365 days. Doesn't sound like that big of a deal, but it was the difference between nothing to look forward to and a light at the end of the tunnel—once a month for Matthew and for us.

I've always thought there must be a special place in heaven reserved for school bus drivers. Just think about the place reserved for a woman who drove a school bus for children with a variety of disabilities every day of the week and then spent one of her days off with a boy who also had some significant needs.

Thank you, Donna, for all that you did for us. I don't know if you can truly appreciate what you gave to my entire family. You gave all of us a day when we could do "normal" activities and gave Matthew respect, fun and so much more. Those Saturdays were wonderful for all of us. We knew that our son was with someone we could trust and who he truly enjoyed being with, doing activities that he loved doing. We *lived* for those Saturdays. It was those Saturdays that allowed every member of my family to get through all the other days in the month.

We *all* thank you!

- 5 -

WHAT CAN WE DO
DURING A RAGE EPISODE?

Obviously everyone's situation is different, but from my experience—not much! It's similar to asking what can be done to make someone sober when he is drunk. You do what you can to keep people safe and wait for the brain chemistry to return to normal. The more important question is: What can we do to prevent the rage?

I can share what I have learned, but these are only my thoughts—they're not written in stone and categorically not right for everyone. Heck, we never found an answer that worked consistently for us. But I can share what we found that didn't work, and some things that worked a little. Take away from this what makes sense for you, knowing that every child is unique, every family is unique and every situation can be unique.

The first major step was that I finally accepted the rage as not being Matthew's or my fault. I also gave myself permission to ignore the typical parenting models that involved rewards and punishments. I needed to come to a place where I believed absolutely that the rage was caused by the complex balance of brain chemistry. These changes were necessary for me to stop taking the violence and abusive rage personally. When I saw my son's challenging behaviors as personal attacks, the natural reaction was anger, which led to threats and punishment.

Not taking symptoms personally was, for me, critical in my attempts at remaining calm. I was better at being curious regarding what might have initiated the rage, and what might be helpful to prevent it next time. This significantly increased my ability to assist in defusing the situation rather than to engage in the rage. I say "attempts" because I wasn't always successful; it's very hard. But once I truly believed that Matthew hated the rage as much, if not more, than I did, it became easier to not take the rage personally. This allowed me to be more available to help my son.

I was told by many people to punish him more; to get in his face and be bigger and louder. This definitely didn't work. I couldn't frighten Matthew out of this rage. I couldn't bully him into submission. Yelling louder didn't help me regain the position of a parent that deserved respect. I have heard many times, "but then doesn't he win?" *No one wins* in these situations! I needed to put aside the idea of either of us "winning."

I also heard, "but then aren't you enabling him?" Is it enabling, or is it supporting a child with an extremely complex disorder? I finally saw that I needed to support Matthew instead of continuing to punish when clearly that did not work.

What to do? I learned that the most important thing was to keep people safe. If that meant I left a full grocery cart in the middle of the store as I followed him running out of the store, it was okay. If it meant that I swallowed my pride and stopped caring what other people thought about me, that was okay as well. If it meant putting locks on every door, that was also okay.

This requires a great deal of patience—something that isn't my strong suit. I used to have a sign on my mirror, "Please give me patience…*Now!*" Change doesn't happen quickly. But when I started to pay attention instead of jumping to a knee jerk parental reaction, I found that I learned much faster what *not* to do. What *to* do was more difficult.

I encourage parents to be detectives and gather clues that may help to prevent or reduce the likelihood of rage occurring in the future. I know this seems impossible, but thinking outside the box can sometimes be helpful. When Matthew got home from school, determining what might help reduce some of the anxiety that built up all day and then allowing him to *do* it was a major step. Allowing him to chill by watching TV; letting him drum without insisting that he practice his lessons, being alright with him smashing a metal trash can lid with a baseball bat were all important. We needed to be open to parenting in a manner that wasn't typical.

I researched the minimal resources that were available back then. I also attended Ross Greene and Rick Lavoie conferences. They were both extremely influential in my discovering alternative ways of parenting that were helpful:

Be curious. This was important even when it didn't make a lot of sense. As an example, Tony, Matthew and I were enjoying a beautiful day outside doing yard work when Matthew decided to bleach our deck so he could re-stain it. Suddenly his tics and anger were off the charts. It was such a rapid and drastic change he asked me what had happened. I told him that I didn't know but since he had been using a strong bleach solution, I suggested he take a shower and put the clothes in the basement. When he was done, he asked me if I noticed a difference. What a difference! His symptoms were quiet again. We stopped using bleach and switched to fragrance free laundry detergent.

Choose your battles carefully. I needed to consider whether something was important enough that it warranted a possible meltdown or rage episode. There is a phrase, "Is this a hill you are willing to die on?" Was Matthew having a cookie before dinner really worth a two-or-three-hour rage? Was my yelling at him for what I perceived to be another example of disrespect really worth the ensuing rage—especially since it never helped in the past?

Consider what *your* issues are and what you can set aside. Having my son call me names was something I *never* imagined I would simply ignore—but I learned to overlook what were manifestations of his symptoms and beyond his control. Life got much better for everyone when I was truly able to do this!

Do whatever you need to do to keep everyone safe. I hesitate to include this. Not only is this pretty obvious, it reminds me of a story when Matthew was in residential placement that is so odd it's also humorous. One day I went to pick him up for a weekend. A young social worker told me that if he got out of control during the weekend I should call her and she would "walk me through it."

The second day home, something set off a rage. I picked up the phone to call the social worker but when Matt saw what I was doing, the rage got even worse. He tried to hit me, kick me and rip the phone off the wall. When she answered the phone, she said, "Mrs. Giordano, is that Matthew I hear?" When I said yes, she said, "Mrs. Giordano, do whatever you need to do to get him under control." I held the phone at arm's length thinking, so this is walking me through it? If I *was* able to do *anything* to get him under control, why on earth would I have placed him in their residential placement? Didn't they realize by now that I couldn't do *anything* and if I could, I certainly would?

So if there is anything that can be done to get your child under control, and it's safe, do it. Additionally, keep trying different strategies when the rage first begins. Pay attention to what works and what doesn't.

Be creative. Try different approaches, no matter how bizarre, that encourage calm with your child. Listen to suggestions that your child may have.

Remember that the rage is the disability and not your child. Try very hard to not take symptoms personally. It gets in the way of being open to strategies that will help your child to manage the symptoms.

Know that this experience is exhausting for everyone. When your child apologizes, accept it even if you are still angry. It was okay for me to be angry; it was never okay to have Matthew think that I loved him less because of his symptoms. If there is one component that I found to be critical, it was that Matthew never doubted my love. We have had some rough moments and life remains bumpy, but we both know without a shadow of a doubt that I love him and he loves me. No question—that is an absolute truth.

MATTHEW'S SERVICE COORDINATORS

We received the support of service coordinators through an agency funded by New York State. We were fortunate that they all got to know Matthew, respected him, recognized his potential and provided the support that he deserved and resulted in him being successful.

One service coordinator, years after she no longer worked with him, sent him an article about events that were springing up in California called drum circles. This article was the inspiration for Matthew initiating his business, Drum Echoes, Inc.

We were fortunate that all of his service coordinators looked past his symptoms, saw him as an individual and helped him recognize and develop his abilities. They taught him strategies specific to his needs so that he could be an independent, successful adult. We thank all of you!

- 6 -

RESIDENTIAL PLACEMENT

The first day we brought Matthew to the Rochester Children's Psychiatric Center (RPC), we were told that we were not allowed to have any contact with our eight year old son for one month: None: no phone calls, no visits, no letters…nothing! I was shocked, felt deep sadness and thought this was just plain wrong. He was my little boy. It just didn't make sense that his mother couldn't visit him or contact him in some way.

So my first lesson in working with—or maybe I should say working around—a system that doesn't always respect parents had begun. I discovered that while the day staff would not allow me anywhere close, no matter what I tried, the evening staff enjoyed homemade cookies. So a few times every week, after dinner I would drive the 45 minutes to RPC with cookies and an item of clothing, a toy or book that I told them Matthew needed.

Whenever the bell rang to the children's unit, all the kids would run to the door to see who was there. So, not only would I get a glimpse of my son, but more importantly, Matthew would see me and know that I had not deserted him. I was still his mother and continued to love him and be there for him. I believe that this consistent and regular contact with him was extremely important for both of us; even if it was less than 1 minute. He saw me; I saw him.

Before bringing Matthew there, I purchased a mommy gorilla stuffed toy with long arms and Velcro at the end of each arm. The mommy gorilla was holding onto her much smaller baby gorilla. I gave this to Matthew and told him that whenever he missed me, even though I couldn't be there myself, my love would always be with him. He could hold them as a reminder of how much we loved each other. Even though we weren't together, we could give each other a hug and our love.

The night before he entered RPC, I brought him outside on our porch and we looked up at the moon. I told him that no matter where we were for the rest of our lives, we would both be looking at the same moon. I promised him that I would ask what time he would be going to bed, and every night I would be looking at the moon at that time. I would be giving him a kiss and a hug and telling him how much I loved him. We would still be together.

Soon after, a movie titled "An American Tale" was released with a theme song titled "Somewhere Out There." It was a cartoon about two mice looking at the moon, knowing that their love kept them together even though they were separated. Matthew recently sent me a link to a short clip of that movie with the little mouse, Fievel, singing the song to the moon. I cried watching that clip even though it was over 20 years since we stood on our porch.

I missed Matthew so much every single day, all day; but particularly at night when the moon came up.

I don't remember much about the process of placing him at RPC, but the intake interview at the second residential placement remains vivid in my memory. Two men introduced themselves as social workers. At the time, I assumed that all social workers were nice people, so I tried to convince myself that this interview wouldn't be too bad. Wrong again!

One of them asked, "So Matthew, who is to blame for your violent behavior?"

"Huh?"

"You know, when you are angry and become violent, breaking windows, trying to hurt people in your family—whose fault is this?" (Silence)

"Is it yours?" (Silence)

"Is it your mother's?" (Silence)

"Is it your father's?" (Silence)

"Who is to blame?"

Matt turned toward me with a look that asked who this person was and what planet he was from; certainly not ours. I didn't say anything because I didn't want to give the slightest hint that I was influencing his answers, especially to a question like that. After repeating the questions and much urging on this man's part, my nine year old little boy finally said to him, "I have Tourette syndrome and it isn't anybody's fault." Oh, the wisdom of a child in the face of adult false assumptions.

The body language of both men communicated clearly, "Yeah, right."

These types of questions went on for another 30 minutes. They finally said that we were done and they would let me know in a week or two if Matthew would be accepted there as a patient.

As we walked toward the parking lot, Matthew looked up at me and said, "I don't like it here and I never want to come back." All I could say was, "I know. I feel the same way." But as it turned out, we did go back because we had no choice.

Having our son live in residential placements was intolerable and impossible to describe adequately to people who have not experienced it. It was surreal; beyond anything I could ever have imagined would be a part of my life. Some people think they can relate, but they can't; not unless you've experienced it. Incredibly, soon after he was there, a woman told me that she understood how I felt because she remembered how difficult it was to leave her son at summer camp. Summer Camp? A children's psychiatric center? Hmmmmmm.

I am reminded of Linda, a woman with whom I work. Her daughter was born with a disability that results in tumors, even on her brain. After five months of believing that medications would work, Linda had to make an anguished decision. She had to choose whether to have surgery on her little baby to remove a portion of her brain. She decided to do it because she was convinced that this would result in a better quality of life not just for her daughter, but for her entire family.

I'm not comparing the two, because I have never experienced anything even close to that. I share it with you as an example of situations in which parents need to make a decision between two dreadful and totally unacceptable choices. There was no clear correct choice and certainly no *good* choice for her. Similarly, there was no clear correct and good choice for Matthew back then. The choice was either him remaining at home and praying that no one was seriously hurt or bring him to live somewhere else. Both options were atrocious.

People have asked me if placing my son was worth it; would I have done it if I knew back then what I know now? My only response is a pain-filled answer that we had no choice. I would have given my life for Matthew if that would have helped him. But I knew absolutely that I could not allow an environment to continue in which there was the possibility that someone could be seriously injured. That was not acceptable on many levels and for obvious reasons. Also, I was confident that if he had seriously hurt someone, it would have destroyed his life. I had to protect Matthew as well as my other children.

It amazes me to read or hear people say or imply in some manner that some parents can't cope so they "send their child away." S*end their child away*? What an incredibly insensitive statement! I have heard different ways to express this over the years. But it all boils down to the same thing—judgmental statements by people who have not lived our lives. When people say this, it indicates that they have no concept of how difficult it can be every minute, every hour, every day, every week, every month, every year, for every person in the family but mostly for the child for whom it is necessary to live away from his family and his home. It's not a good choice—it isn't even an acceptable choice; but it was our *only* choice.

"I know that you are not the type of mother who would ever put your son away in one of those places." That was the statement said to me approximately two weeks before my husband and I placed our son at the Children's Unit of RPC.

I wanted to ask this man exactly what type of mother was he referring to?! Was he suggesting that the "type of mother" who would do that is a mother who doesn't love her child enough and thinks that taking care of her child is just too much trouble? Is it the mother who just can't be bothered anymore?

Or is it a mother who loves her child *so much* that she would do anything—*anything*—regardless of how unthinkable and painful, in order to protect her child? Is it a mother who knows that to save her child's life, they must live apart for a time? Is it a mother who cares so much that she will allow other people to provide the care that she so desperately wants to give to her little boy? Is it a mother who lives every day and every moment with the fear that something awful will happen to her son while he is not with her? Fear from knowing that people who are responsible for his well-being are employees who don't know him, don't love him and are most likely underpaid. At the same time knowing that there was no other option.

A few years ago, I was enjoying dinner with a close friend, my daughter, Erika and Dan, my future son-in-law. Dan asked if I was aware of the controversy that involved a boy who was in a mental health residential setting and died from inappropriate and over-zealous restraints. Immediately after this story broke, he explained, there was an on-going and lengthy debate in the local newspaper's editorial pages regarding why any parent would "send their child to live in a place like that."

We all found it incredible that people would take the time and effort involved in writing to the newspaper to place blame on parents they didn't know and had no idea what their life was like. Does it somehow make people feel like they are better parents? Is it because our society wants answers and this is an attempt at providing a quick and easy place to put the blame? Would the discussion be the same if instead of being in a residential setting, the child were in a hospital for an extended stay to receive the necessary treatment for cancer? I don't think so.

Parents are such an easy target. Instead of blaming the parents for this child's death, it seems more appropriate to recognize that our system of providing care to children with mental health issues is broken. People working with our children are sometimes untrained and highly underpaid. Was this the fault of the parent or the fault of a society that underfunds the mental health system designed to provide care to children?

Many people ask me if there was one incident that made me see there was no option for my family other than residential placement. I can only say that it was a culmination of escalating and very serious and dangerous events. So let's go back and talk about how Tony and I came to this decision. What were our lives like that led us to making such a painful and unthinkable decision?

We had arranged for Matthew to attend a week-long Tourette syndrome camp the summer he turned eight years old. It was held in another state. We knew that getting him there would be a three-to-four-hour trip from hell because of the consistent and horrific difficulties he always had when riding in a car. We believed it was worth it because being with other children who had Tourette might help him in some way. Additionally, we had decided to use this time as a vacation with our other children who were often not receiving the time and attention they deserved. My family needed a break and I honestly thought Matthew would have a good time and possibly come home better.

I was confident that everything would go well because he would be in a safe and accepting environment with other children who were similar. I had been assured that the counselors were trained to understand and support children with Tourette syndrome. Once again, I was hopeful of finding an answer for this disorder. Who knows, possibly having him spend a week there would magically result in reducing symptoms and eliminating the neurological rage.

Matthew had a decent time at camp, but we didn't find our answer. Like many experiences, however, the week unexpectedly provided us with important information that would impact our lives significantly. I missed him terribly during that week, but to my surprise, that brief respite allowed me to recognize how unnormal our lives were. We were living with aggression and violence which had begun slowly and had escalated to become 'the norm' in our home. We had lost sight of how out of whack things were. It wasn't as if we had been a *normal* American family one week and the next a family with a child whose symptoms were abusive and violent two-to-three hours every day.

Instead, we were somehow unaware of the severity of our situation because it started small and had grown in frequency and intensity over a two year period. It's similar to physical pain. There is a major difference between breaking a leg and having a minor pain becoming more intense over time. Our minds somehow manage to adapt to the growing pain resulting in it being somehow tolerable. We had lost all sense of *normal* because it no longer existed in our home.

Matthew hitting his sister every time she sniffed, which was her tic, became normal. Enduring a two-hour episode of screaming, swearing, breaking things because something had not been done "right"; swearing at his father for "breathing"; throwing and breaking things, kicking holes in the walls, had all become sort of *normal*.

At the end of the week, I couldn't wait to pick him up from the camp; to see that he was safe and to hug him. I loved my son and wanted to hold him and tell him how much I loved him. At the same time, I couldn't ignore that in his absence, the rest of my family was experiencing a *normalcy* for the first time in years.

Soon after returning home from camp, he and I stopped at a store and Matthew asked for a candy bar. My refusal resulted in another broken windshield. After yet another dangerous ride home, I called the pediatric neurological social worker. I struggled with the huge lump in my throat as I told her about what had occurred and that clearly, I had no control over my little boy.

Later that same day, he was upset with me for preventing him from hitting his brother in order to complete the *need* for getting the *last touch*. He took my hand and told me to come with him. He brought me to the top of the stairs, got behind me and tried to push me down. Fortunately, I knew enough to be holding onto the railing. I turned to him and said, "You could have killed mommy." He said, "I wanted to kill you."

A few minutes later, he was sobbing uncontrollably and told me he wanted to die. He asked me why he did these awful things.

That same day, I was sitting out on our front porch steps feeling overwhelmed, not knowing what to do for my son and feeling totally helpless. I heard Matthew call my name and when I turned around, he hit me with the dog's metal water bowl. I never went to the hospital for treatment because I was afraid that if they knew what had happened, they would contact Child Protective Services or even the police. I was terrified of what would happen if people knew what was occurring behind our doors.

Shortly after that, I walked into the kitchen and my little boy was holding a large knife to his chest. He wanted to die because he hated himself for what he had done. He was very aware of the pain he was causing the family that he loved so much. He asked me why God hated him and made him do these bad things. My little boy looked at me and said that everyone would be happier if he just died. I held him in my arms and told him that it would be the saddest day of my life if he died. I would cry every day if I didn't see his smile, hear his laughter and his drumming. I talked about all the people who loved him and would be sad if he were not in their lives. I asked him who would bring me flowers; who would I be able to read stories to because Erika and Jeff were too old for that. He laughed a little.

I knew he was serious and it scared me to the depth of my being.

I confided to my therapist the terrifying details. She asked me to consider what it would do to Matthew if he either accidentally killed or permanently damaged a sibling, his father, or more likely, his mother. It was clear, beyond a shadow of a doubt, that if he ever did seriously hurt someone, he would not be able to live with this guilt. I knew he would kill himself. I was desperate to protect him. Desperate and needing to do something quickly.

These were the slaps of reality that I needed to recognize that no matter how hard I tried, I was not finding how to help my son and in the meantime I was putting everyone, including Matthew, at severe risk.

I called the social worker again. I kept saying to her over and over that I didn't know what to do. She was familiar with our lives and knew that in spite of a loving family, the situation was desperate and dangerous. She knew that nothing I did would make any difference in Matthew's behavior. She was very aware that any punishment would not prevent him from repeating similar behaviors, and that threats and punishment only increased the level of violence and danger at that moment. When Matthew was in a rage state there was *nothing...nothing* that could be done. People who have not lived through a similar experience with their child cannot understand how this can be true. Fortunately, Joan believed me.

She called me two days later to tell me that she had some good news. She had managed to get us an appointment at the Rochester Psychiatric Center Children's Unit for an intake interview. She asked, "How does that sound?" I said, "I think that sounds like hell."

How could this be good for *my* little boy who brought me bouquets of wild flowers and gave me so much joy with his delightful ways of interacting with people, animals and nature?

How could this be a good idea for *my* little boy, who was a sponge for information on almost any topic, could make such incredibly beautiful music and tell us in so many ways how much he loved us.

Poor Joan! I'm sure that she called in many favors for us to get an appointment for an intake that quickly. I'm sure that she expected me to be pleased and grateful. I quickly realized that I had to make one of those unthinkable decisions. Do I accept help from professionals who have experience working with children?

Or do we continue to keep him at home, praying that his neurological imbalance wouldn't result in someone being seriously hurt or killed?

We also needed to consider how our inability to control outbursts that resulted in dangerous behaviors would impact his emotional well-being. Would he believe that he was a bad person and a danger to the family that he loves? What would be the long term impact? Matthew was always extremely remorseful when there was an episode and always apologized. He would say that he was evil and ask me, "Why does God hate me? Why did he make me like this?" Every time he asked me that same question, it tore at my heart. I would hold my little boy in my arms and tell him how much we all loved him. I needed Matthew to know that as his parents we would do anything, *Anything*, to keep him safe and to keep him from hurting others no matter how painfully difficult it was for all of us. At the time, he was a young boy and, of course, he didn't understand.

We made the appointment to visit the facility and speak to the doctors and therapists.

I was overcome with despair and disbelief when I saw that the children's psychiatric hospital was housed in a building that was built in the early 1920s. There were bars on the windows and a mammoth door that had to be unlocked with keys held on a large ring—just like in the movies. We heard the keys jingling from the other side of the door when we rang the bell. After entering the main door, if you turned to the left, you entered the facility for the adult criminally insane. If you turned to the right, you entered the facility for children. I can't imagine how anyone thought this was a good plan. It scared me to the depth of my soul.

In the end, it had to be Matthew who needed to discover a way to never hurt anyone, and somehow he did this. I don't know how and I'll never know the pain he endured to do this. He developed strategies so that causing physical harm to others was no longer an issue. I'm not saying that this was a result of him being taught something during the four years he was in residential care. I believe it was completely a result of *his* determination to live at home safely with his family.

How does a child who is so young do this? I don't know, but I do know that he did it. The last time we worried about violence was prior to him being 12 years old. That was over 17 years ago and that part of his disability is gone. Yes, he had medications, and therapists, but I believe that he found the answer for that part of the puzzle himself. He was provided strategies, but it was Matthew who was driven to find what worked for him.

For instance, hitting Erika's arm when she sniffed was a major problem. So, it was agreed that if Matthew touched Erika in any way after she sniffed, no matter where we were, he needed to return to RPC immediately. Our first outing from RPC as a family finally arrived. We went bowling during the two hours he was permitted to be with us. We were there for only ten minutes before Erika sniffed. Matthew walked by her and casually bumped into her. I was horrified. I knew that we needed to bring him back—no discussion.

We brought him back.

When we got home, I walked into the woods, fell to my knees and sobbed until I was gasping for air.

It took some time and I don't know how, but Matthew somehow figured out how to manage this symptom. Instead of hitting her, whenever Erika sniffed he would say, "Shit, Erika." Considering the two options, hitting or "Shit, Erika?" Not even close. I could handle "Shit, Erika." This was the first of many strategies he developed to manage his symptoms.

We brought him home every weekend we were allowed. Every time we brought him back, I asked myself the same question: How could we be doing this? After all, when he wasn't in a neurological rage, he was fun, bright, gentle and loving—just a sweet and wonderful little boy. But I could never for a minute ignore the rage that was dangerous for everyone in my family, but primarily for Matthew. When it came time on Sundays for him to return to RPC, my insides screamed, "I just can't do this anymore." But we had no choice.

With his hand in my hand, we walked past the barbed wire, through the doors, pushed a buzzer and waited. We waited to hear the jangle of keys as the inner door was opened. We walked him to his room, gave him a hug and kiss, turned and walked away. Sometimes he would cling to us and the attendants had to hold him back crying, and begging us not to leave him there. I had to continuously remind myself and with much determination, that no matter what, I needed to protect him!

The second placement, Crestwood Children's Center, was a major improvement over the first. There was grass, separate and individual buildings that didn't look like jails, no barbed wire and not even a fence—it was in a rural setting which was a significant difference.

For the most part, the staff was incredibly supportive of our son. Many of them sincerely accepted him for who he was, including his strengths, his difficulties, and his complex disorder. I know for a fact that some of them truly tried to help him in creative ways because they saw his abilities and his frustrations.

One young man, Jodi, was with him on the day that I picked Matthew up to bring him to his next placement. He walked Matthew out to my car and when my son turned to say goodbye, Jodi picked him up and they hugged for a full two minutes. I sat in the car crying because clearly this young man cared about my son and Matthew was sad to be saying goodbye to his friend. Jodi made a lasting impression on his life. He recognized Matthew as a boy who was dealing with difficulties and not as a "difficult child." He had treated him with the respect that all children deserve and need.

Matthew was at RPC for over a year and at Crestwood for six months. To say that this was a difficult time for all of us is a major understatement. When he was nine, he told me repeatedly that I couldn't possibly be his *real* mother because a *real* mother would never do that to her child. Of course he felt that way—he was a child and wanted more than anything to be at home where he belonged.

I had feared that Matthew would hate me forever for bringing him to residential placements and that he would never get past the feeling of desertion. I was afraid that he would never forgive me. How would I be able to live with that?

I, of course, recognize why people see placing a child in a psychiatric center as an unimaginable decision. I once shared the belief that there must be a different or better option. It was inconceivable to me that I would ever be a parent who would remove my son from his home and family. It continues to be inconceivable even as I write this, and still makes my gut twist and turn. I loved my son then; I love him now and have never stopped believing in his kindness and potential.

I was recently thinking about those awful years. Matthew must have seen my sadness because he put his arm across my shoulders and told me that he knew how hard it must have been for me to bring him to the placements. He said he understood that I had to do it because he wouldn't have been able to live with himself if he had done something terrible to me or someone else. He has said that to me many times over the years. This particular time, he added something that I will always hold in my heart. He told me that all the time he was out of the home, he felt himself being surrounded by my love and my presence. He knew I loved him and he never doubted it.

I understand, however, that there are times when he struggles with the feelings that were prominent as a child. He knows that I did it because I love him and he needed help; but he also has that little eight year old boy inside him who couldn't understand how his mother did this to him. He felt deserted—of course he did; he was a little, little boy.

DR. EMAMI, SENIOR PSYCHIATRIST

Dr. Emami has a remarkable passion for helping children who are most in need of help. Amazingly, he also does not rely on the common practice of blaming parents. He is one of the most respected child therapists in the area, yet he has dedicated his life to children in residential placements.

When first introduced, I was surprised and somewhat amused, in a sad way, that the person who would be in charge of my son's care had a name that was pronounced 'a-mommy.' He is a gentle, extremely wise, caring and quiet man who assisted Matthew by being open-minded to this little boy's misunderstood symptoms. He believed my son and came to respect and understand my husband and me when many other therapists had a difficult time doing so. It's possible that he may have secretly thought that it was our fault when we first met, but I don't remember sensing that from him. Instead I only experienced his respect for us as parents and a family.

Thank you, Dr. Emami, for your belief in my son, your openness to having a mutually respectful relationship with Tony and me, and for having a truly honest, supportive and even loving relationship with Matthew. I will never forget the day Matthew left RPC. You told Tony and me that it wasn't our fault and that Matthew needed to be there. You said that even if he were your child, that he would've still needed to go to RPC. When Matt came to your office to say goodbye, you hugged him and promised that if he ever needed to see you again, no matter how long it had been, you would see him. Many years later, you kept that promise. Thank you, Dr. Emami, for everything.

- 7 -

FOSTER PLACEMENT

Foster placement began for Matthew when Crestwood told us that it was no longer appropriate for him to remain there. They told us we had a choice. We could either bring him home or place him in a therapeutic foster home. I had never heard of therapeutic foster care and didn't know how this differed from regular foster care. So, I talked with people I knew in Social Services who told me that it involved couples that were trained in mental health difficulties. I was assured they would receive ongoing training and support from mental health professionals as long as the child was in their home. It also meant that there would be no other children with difficult behaviors living there.

The placement that had been chosen was with a couple who lived in the same school district as us. Matthew's therapist, Tony and I all agreed that this would be best for him. The assurance that the foster parents would receive ongoing training, would have support from mental health providers and that Matthew would attend his home school, provided at least some positive aspects to this otherwise unbearable thought. We decided to meet the couple and consider this option.

A meeting was scheduled for us to meet the foster parents to be held in at Crestwood, where Matthew was living. Tony and I wanted to make sure that everyone knew we would absolutely continue to be very involved in his life. We would bring him to doctor appointments, to drum lessons, family gatherings and home for weekends. He could call us on the phone and we would be able to call him. Everything was agreed to and seemed okay— not *great* by any stretch of the imagination, but sort of doable—

particularly since we, once again, didn't have any other realistic option.

One of the social workers asked if we would like to go ahead with the placement. Tony and I said that we would. They asked the foster parents if they were ready to meet Matthew.

The punched-in-the-stomach reality hit me. The *oth*er reason for the meeting that evening was so that the foster parents could meet him to determine if they felt that it was "a good fit." What had never occurred to me was that *they might not approve of him*!

It made sense in retrospect but I had never for an instant considered the possibility that they would "reject" our son. This is my son! My child!…How could anyone *reject him*?

Someone asked me if I would like to "retrieve" Matthew from the cottage or if one of them should. I was stunned! RETRIEVE? Why do people in these situations use words that are so inhuman? I don't remember ever being asked to *retrieve* any of my other children.

The entire experience reminded me of times when I have adopted a dog at the local animal center. An attendant would walk out back to "retrieve" the dog so we could determine if we were compatible and whether it was *a good fit*. Was this what I was doing with my son?

Was I really walking to bring my son back to determine if he was acceptable to these people? The moment was surreal. This is not what a mother does with her 10 year old son. No way did this fit into my world. No way—no way; absolutely *no way!*

But somewhere in my emotionally numbed brain, I knew that this was something that needed to happen. I tried to extinguish the pain that was ripping my insides apart and my strong desire to gather up my son and get the hell out of there. Instead, I told them that I was his mother and I needed to be the one that would go get Matthew.

So, once again, I had to do what I found to be unthinkable. I went to his cottage and asked him to come with me. I will never forget that walk. My legs were limp and it felt as if I was trudging through thick, deep, sticky mud. Every step took astounding effort. I remember needing to tell myself as I walked, right foot, left foot; right foot, left foot…

I don't recall if we talked as we walked back to the building where everyone waited. I suspect that we did. Matthew has always been very social and talked at every opportunity with anyone who was available. We hadn't seen each other for a few days so I would guess that we chatted. About what? I have no clue. I may have mustered up some enthusiasm regarding how this was a positive move towards coming home for good.

Either these people would reject my son or they would agree to take him into their home—into their family. I was numb. How does any of this make sense? How is any of this what should be happening to him, to us, to our family? How is this real? How had we gotten to this moment? To this place? How could I take another step? How could I possibly explain this to him? How could he ever forgive me for doing this?

As Matthew and I entered the room, I didn't know if I wanted him to be his charming self or to have an explosion so they would not want him. After what seemed like an eternity, the meeting ended and I brought him back to the cottage. He had been delightful—they accepted him.

We were given the papers that we needed to sign if our son was going to receive the services he required; the papers that would allow the county to assume custody of our son.

Later that night, the truth struck me as nothing I had ever experienced before or since. Another woman had the job of being my 10 year old son's "mother." She would be there to comfort him when he skinned his knee; she would tuck him in at night and wake him in the morning. He would talk with her about his day in school. She would be the one to cook his meals and help him with his homework. She would give him hugs when he was sad, she would hear him laugh and be silly. She would be acting as his "mom."

I could barely breathe. I drove around not knowing what to do or where to go. I wanted to go 'away'—far, far away. More than anything I wanted to drive to my therapist's house because I was certain that she could help me make sense of this. I didn't care that it was night time and her time off. She would hold me and let me cry and not try to find something good to say or try to 'fix it.' She would let me *feel* the overwhelming and crushing sadness that I couldn't numb myself to no matter how I tried. I called her house but she wasn't home. So instead, I struggled harder at not feeling the anguish that was breaking my heart.

The two years that Matthew was in foster care are not easy to talk about, let alone explain. It began with the papers that we were required to sign.

The forms included a list of reasons why Social Services could permanently remove our parental rights. The first reason listed was for not participating in therapy sessions that we were required to attend. Next was if we did not visit our son at the designated times. These didn't bother me because, of *course,* we would visit him.

There were, however, provisions for which I had major problems. One was that we would not be notified when our son had a doctor's appointment; another was that the foster parents would determine the best medications and therapeutic interventions. Additionally, it would not be necessary for us to be at school meetings. As I read this list, I felt anger, sadness, but mostly agonizing fear deep in my gut.

But the specification that pulled the plug on my heart was the very last. It stated that our parental rights would be permanently removed "for any reason that Social Services would deem to be in the best interest of the child." *Any* reason that *they* deemed to be in the best interest of *my* child!

I couldn't sign this paper. I spoke to some friends of mine, and finally to an attorney to whom I paid more money than I could afford at the time. This attorney was recommended by a friend who knew her as a past social worker that had worked at Social Services in the Foster Care Program. After a brief discussion, she told me that I needn't be afraid of them taking away my son and that in reality they didn't *want* my son. She said that she had never seen a child removed from parents as involved and committed to their child as we were. She added that since it was a legal contract, she didn't see any reason why *we* couldn't add some stipulations of our own.

So we added addendums that said we would bring our son to the doctor's and make decisions regarding medications and education. We would bring him to his drum lessons and visit him after calling first to see if that was convenient. The director of the Foster Care Program at Social Services told us they had never been anything like this; told us what an *interesting* family we were, but they accepted it.

All those words: foster child, foster parents, foster home, foster sister, foster brother, and the worst—foster Mom and foster Dad. All those words that didn't belong in our world. All those words that made no sense to me. He had only one Mom—ME. He had only one father—TONY. He had only one brother— JEFF, and one sister—ERIKA. His home was at our house; our home. We were his parents and he was our son.

The day came for Matthew to move into the foster home. His Social Services worker told me that she would bring him there. Again, I felt that this was *my* job, so I told her I would pick him up and bring him to their house.

I tried to act upbeat while I was driving there and while we were in their house. As I was preparing to leave, I talked to the family's mother. Her son called out, "Mom, can I have a piece of candy?" Then I heard Matthew similarly call out "Mom?" I turned and said, "Yes?" He said, "Not you, my other Mom." Those words, even 20 years later, are still difficult to even type.

I left quickly because I didn't want Matthew to see that those words had made my insides crumble.

I saw Matthew's therapist the next day and I asked about him saying that. She explained that it had been two years since he had lived in a home—any home. He just wanted to fit in some place; to fit in with a family—any family. And that was why he called her 'mom.' I guess that made sense, and did ease the pain…somewhat.

I never said anything to Matthew about it. The next time I saw him was at their house. He called her by her first name, and to my knowledge, that was the only time he called someone else "mom."

I met with Social Services on a regular basis and discussed my discomfort with the words "Foster mother and father; foster sister and brother; foster home." Words have power and I hated these words. I would do whatever I could to erase them from my world.

I told them that Matthew could call these people whatever he felt comfortable calling them. But when the social workers met with us, they would never use those words. I suggested that when meeting with me, that they use the words 'foster providers' and 'foster placement'—*always* when they were speaking to me. Nothing different…ever!

Everything about his foster placement was difficult, even interactions with strangers who were involved in our lives during that time. Unfortunately, people make assumptions regarding a parent that would need their child in foster care. One day I picked up Matthew to bring him to see a new therapist. The receptionist asked if I were the "biological Mom." BIOLOGICAL MOM!?!

She didn't mean to inflict the pain that felt like someone had stomped on my chest, but she did. I looked at her and said, "I am his mother. I am the only mother he has ever had. I am the only mother he will *ever* have."

Assumptions! People so easily make assumptions regarding parents and children. People that know you, family members, strangers, school personnel, providers can all make assumptions about symptoms that appear to be purposeful behaviors and assumptions regarding parents that allow their child to 'act like that.' I hate assumptions!

Matthew stayed in the foster placement from 10 to 12 years old. Two years, which were the most difficult of all of his placements—at least for me. My son living in a residential setting was similar to having my child in a hospital; painful, but I could rationalize that it was a hospital and was for his welfare and his health. Having my son live with another family was agonizing for me every single day, particularly when I saw him at the grocery store or a school event and when he left to go with them.

Finally, the day came for Matthew to come home for good. It was his father's idea to surprise him by renting a limousine. His older brother, best friend and cousin would already be in the limo when it arrived to pick him up. As a surprise, we invited our neighbors and friends to be at our house when he arrived home. It was a fabulous day!

Years later, I asked Tony how he was able to sign those papers so easily. He told me he never believed what he was signing. As he signed it, he knew that if it ever became necessary, we would take Matthew along with the rest of the family and disappear. He would never turn over his son. I had thought precisely the same but we had never talked about it with each other.

Foster placement, is without a doubt, extremely difficult— but like many other difficult decisions, for the sake of our son, we had no choice.

SHERIFF MELONI

When Matthew was eight years old, Sheriff Meloni began as his Compeer volunteer. He had been at the RPC for about six months when Dr. Emami talked to us about a Compeer Program that matched adults with children to spend quality time together. We thought it sounded very positive, but told him that we would need to be involved in choosing the person who would be teamed up with our son. Dr. Emami looked at me with a grin and said that it was Sheriff Meloni. At the time, he was the most famous, well-liked and respected person in the Rochester region. Incredibly, another amazing person fell into our lives.

One of the places that Sheriff Meloni took Matthew when they were together was the local mall. They walked around, ate ice cream and enjoyed each other's company. One of the truly valuable influences in Matthew's life was that this man and local celebrity was not embarrassed to walk in public places with him, even when the tics were severe or his vocalizations loud and inappropriate.

Matthew developed a relationship with Sheriff Meloni's entire family that continues to this day. Mrs. Meloni treated him like one of her own children and Matthew reminded me frequently what an incredibly fantastic cook she was. I still see her occasionally around town and she always asks about him; it's easy to see in her eyes how much she cares. Thank you, Sheriff and Mrs. Meloni. As the saying goes, it takes a village to raise a child. Thank you for being in our village.

- 8 -

THE IMPORTANCE OF BALANCE

Picture a Norman Rockwell painting of a town hall built in the late 1800s. The hall is filled with the town's residents sitting on folding chairs and old church pews while people of all ages are on stage singing, playing musical instruments and dancing. Even the members of the volunteer fire department are performing their rendition of "Little Bunny Foo Foo."

This was the scene in which Matthew, at the age of five, had his first drum solo performance. The audience could see only the top of his head from behind the drums. It was the first time we saw audience members' facial expressions change from "Awww, isn't he cute" to "holy mackerel, that kid is *good*."

His interest and talent for percussion instruments first became obvious when Matthew was two. We always had music playing in our house. This particular day, the Moody Blues record "I'm Just a Singer in a Rock-n-Roll Band" was playing on our turntable. I walked into the living room and saw our little boy keeping perfect rhythm while air drumming.

We bought him a $25 child-sized drum set for Christmas. The drum set didn't last long, but it provided us with an opportunity to see his natural talent. Matthew not only enjoyed drumming, but had incredible talent for it as well. For his fourth birthday, we bought him a beginner's drum set. When he wasn't drumming on this or hand drums, he drummed on anything and everything in our house. Fortunately, distressed furniture fit into the décor of our log house.

At five, Matthew began taking lessons from local high school students. One of his young teachers, Shane, went on to be a percussionist for Yo Yo Ma. As an adult, I have heard Matt share with audience members that one of the valuable lessons Shane taught him was to have fun and enjoy the music. After every lesson, they used the last 5 minutes to jam—Matthew on the drum set and Shane on the guitar. Shane knew the importance of his not only learning the mechanics of performing, but also developing a love and a sense of joy for *making* music as well. Thank you, Shane!

When Matthew was eight, we brought him to the Eastman School of Music to meet with Ruth Cahn, who was the lead percussionist for the Rochester Philharmonic Orchestra. She immediately impressed me by speaking directly to Matthew—not his parents. It showed respect for her future student and the fact that her relationship with him was of primary importance. They discussed his love of drumming, and then she played rhythms and asked him to repeat them. After approximately 15 minutes, Ruth looked at Matthew and told him that she would be honored to be his teacher if he were interested in being her student. He enthusiastically said yes as only a youngster can. She was his teacher and he was her student for the next eight years.

What an incredible positive turn of events for our son. Doing an activity that he loved with a highly respected teacher in one of the most famous and glamorous buildings in Rochester. Without realizing it at the time, a critical component of his not being 'disabled' by his significant symptoms was unfolding. His extreme symptoms were balanced by his extraordinary talent. Quite incredibly, however, some of the therapists and counselors who worked with us suggested that if Matthew was *bad* or *inappropriate*, we should take away his drums and his lessons!

I am aware that the common philosophy for raising a child involves punishment. This assumes that not only will the objectionable behavior cease, but it will be replaced with a behavior that society recognizes as acceptable. Let me be clear, there were many times that we punished Matthew, but to take away his drums as punishment seemed ludicrous. His life was extremely difficult, to say the least. His drumming was his joy, his passion and one of the few things in his life that was positive. Why would I want to use it either as a punishment or as a reward?

A young man told one of my co-workers, "Don't ever tell *them* what you like because they will either make you *earn* it or they will *take* it away." This wise statement nails it. What a shame! Instead of adults encouraging a child's strengths as a balance to the difficulties, we make children *earn them or we take them away.*

I guess Matthew may have come by his oppositional behaviors naturally because I became oppositional. I ignored advice that suggested I take his drums away. Instead, we celebrated and nurtured his talents, because it just made sense. By doing this, people saw him not only as a youngster with Tourette syndrome, but also as a gifted drummer. Because other people recognized this, Matthew did as well.

We adults tell children that they are more than just their diagnoses, but I believe we need to practice what we preach. Because of his gift for playing percussion instruments, Matthew was able to have more than a one-sided identity. He was (and is) a great deal more than the person who has a diagnosis of Tourette. He has always had a sense of the importance of balance. I believe it is a critical component of his growing up and becoming the person that he is today.

This 'balance' was most apparent when Matthew was at RPC and taking lessons at the Eastman School. Every Saturday I picked him up at the children's unit and walked past the ever-present reminder of the adult forensic unit being next to the children's facility. I had to walk between the fenced in yard topped with razor wire to my left and the yard with swing sets and slides to my right. Amazing! Matthew constantly asked me if we were bringing him to jail. I still feel the stabbing pain and the tightening of my chest thinking of my son living in this building.

Eastman Theater and RPC. Two such totally different buildings were central to his childhood. One was a building that represented talent, success and self-worth; the other a building that represented isolation, depression and extreme sadness. It was a tangible example of the extremes of Matthew's young life. Incredible talents versus significant symptoms. I picked him up at a depressing and frightening building and brought him to a stunningly beautiful representation of architecture, which housed the talents of musicians from around the world. It was a reminder of the bizarre but extremely important balance for Matthew.

Matthew's symptoms were seen as extreme by everyone who witnessed them. When he drummed, he was respected by adults and his peers while he enjoyed his favorite activity—producing music. He had regular appointments with doctors and therapists who attempted to help reduce his symptoms. Every week he entered this prestigious building to spend an hour learning from one of the most respected percussionists in the area.

I should take this away? I should tell him that if he wasn't 'good' he couldn't go to his lesson; couldn't practice or couldn't play his drums? I was to prevent him from entering this prestigious building that weekly reinforced the fact that he was a member of an exclusive and talented club?

One Saturday morning as we walked through the expansive entrance hall, a young woman in her early twenties said "Hi" to Matthew and *not to me*. She acknowledged Matthew; my nine year old son. I remember thinking that this was due to the fact that *I wasn't* a member of this exclusive group—but he was! It sounds like an unimportant event, but I remember it as one of many moments that would remind me how his talent had such a powerful and positive impact on the way other people viewed him in spite of his symptoms.

I decided early on that the most important job I had as his parent was to get him to adulthood with his self-esteem intact. I wanted him to enter the adult world knowing that he had potential and could accomplish greatness—not to feel like a failure who never did anything right.

While some people told us we should use the drums either as a reward or punishment, others made comments such as "he must practice all the time." They were certain that it must have calmed him when he practiced the drums. I smiled and agreed that he did practice and that it was calming for him. I didn't tell them that while he played the drums frequently, he practiced very little. Yes, his tics were quiet when he played the drums, but that things could also get nasty when his drumming wasn't going "just right."

I am very glad that I decided to disregard professionals when they suggested that I take his drums away. As an adult, Matt not only has good self-esteem, he has an incredibly unique talent from which to make a career. I am committed to the importance of balance. Kids need to know that their diagnoses are only *part* of who they are—and definitely not the most important part.

Many children with these types of difficulties live outside the box and have natural abilities and talents. They often are creative thinkers, writers, artists, musicians, dancers, athletes. Some have the ability to be hyper focused on developing skills, interests and talents. But when their talents are not nurtured, or even worse, when they are used as threats or punishment, the desire to engage in the activity often fades into the background.

These young people have mountains to climb: physical, emotional, social, academic; dating, getting and keeping jobs, finding careers and having a family. Often even everyday activities such as grocery shopping, taking a bus, or going to the movies can be difficult.

They have many struggles, but also may have one area in which they excel. Matthew's experience taught me the importance of putting as much time and energy into developing his strengths as I did into understanding his disorders. Was this tiring and exhausting? Yes—but so incredibly important and rewarding.

Every year the local Moose Club sponsored a talent show for school-aged children, Kindergarten through twelfth grade. They actually had cash prizes! The first year Matthew entered, he was in the senior division, even though he was only in sixth grade. I let friends know that he would be playing his drums in the show, and they asked me who would be playing with him. When I told them that he was doing a solo drum performance, they were confused as to how a drum solo could possibly be entertaining.

Every year, Matthew worked for a month or more on writing, practicing and rewriting his song that he would perform. As he practiced, I heard the various combinations of rhythms. It wasn't until he played in front of the audience that the song came alive and, much to many people's surprise, he created music by playing a drum solo.

That first year, my close friend Brenda attended the show with us. She knew how difficult Matthew's life was. There was also a group of girls from sixth grade sitting in the front rows. During his performance, they screamed as if he were a rock star. At the end of the song, he stood and bowed from the waist as his teachers had taught him. The girls screamed again; so as a true performer, he walked behind his drum set and did an encore drum roll. He is a born entertainer with a natural sense for giving the audience what they want.

That evening there were a few dancers, some singers, four rock bands and Matthew in the show. It came time to announce the winners. Since he was competing against high school students, I wasn't confident that he would win. When they announced Matthew Giordano as first place, Brenda and I both leapt to our feet cheering. I wanted to yell out, "THAT'S MY SON!" The judges had no idea of Matthew's diagnosis or his difficulties; all they knew was that this young boy had blown the audience away with his drumming performance. There were many similar moments over the years and they were all as fantastic as that first time.

Matthew continued to enter these shows until the year he graduated from high school. One year, he said he was thinking about not entering so someone else could win. He wasn't boasting—it really was out of kindness, although I suspect that there may have been a certain girl in the competition who he wanted to win.

Too many children have talent in a specific area and for, some reason or another, are prevented from participating in the activity. For example, there was a young boy who had a natural ability for diving. He also had some major sensory issues and could not endure the sensation of being in the water long enough for him to swim any more than it took to reach the side of the pool after a dive. For him, being in the water longer than that was torture. Last I heard he wasn't diving in any organized group because everywhere he went, they insisted that he must also swim laps to participate in diving; very regrettable for both this young boy and the sport of diving.

We have seen the impact of teaching Matthew the importance of balance in his adult life. For instance, when he was first living on his own, there were times when he found it necessary to call me when he knew he was off-balanced. We developed a code. If when I said hello, he said "evergreen," this was our signal that the briefer this conversation, the better. I made minimal comments and asked only the most necessary of questions.

He would call me later in the day—usually after he had eaten something, exercised, played the drum or just woken up more—and apologize. We then had a more complete conversation. It was important that when this occurred, my focus was on the *strategy* and not why any of this was happening. I didn't ask questions; I didn't take it personally…that is what was and what worked; at least for that moment.

Matthew has never been one dimensional. In order to maintain a balance, all areas of his interests, his talents and symptom must be considered. A close friend of mine once described Matthew as being a beautiful and unique mobile. All mobiles have a delicate balance. If one section of a mobile becomes off-balanced, all of its parts are impacted, resulting in the mobile becoming twisted to the point of becoming nonfunctional. This was also true for Matthew. We learned over the years that he required certain fundamentals to maintain a balance. When he was 'out of balance,' his symptoms increased and he became similar to the twisted mobile, unable to function.

Matthew has learned several components that help him remained balanced. He keeps healthy food available at all times to replenish the calories that his body burns so rapidly.
Next is exercise. We have been told for years that exercise increases those 'good' brain chemicals. He attempts to begin each day with an exercise routine and/or participate in other forms of exercise during the day. Plenty of water is also important. I'm not sure if it cleans out environmental toxins or just keeps his body hydrated (or both), but plenty of water has always been beneficial.

Work is critical for Matt. Lying around and doing nothing for an extended period of time definitely is not good for my son. But this also requires a balance. For instance, when he was young, it became clear that being in school, holding it together, managing symptoms and doing his academic work was often as much as could be expected of him for that day. Requiring additional chores when he got home was way too much for him. As his therapist told me one day, "Matthew's job is to go to school. Doing anything more right now may be asking too much of him."

A good night's sleep is often difficult for Matthew to achieve, but for obvious reasons it's important. Anything that causes stress, physically or emotionally, almost certainly will increase symptoms and there isn't anything much more stressful than being sleep deprived.

Like most of us, friends and family are important for our emotional well-being and balance. It is for Matthew as well. When he decided to drive across the country to live in Denver, I was concerned but not terrified. Being who he is, I was confident that he would develop a new circle of friends fairly easily.

Lastly, everyone who knows Matt recognizes the importance of his making music. I won't say drumming or even percussion instruments. As an explanation, I will quote the Hot Doc International Festival website and Michelle Latimer, describing the premier performance of the documentary "75 Watts":

"Eclectic drummer Matt Giordano describes his body as a 75-watt light bulb that's been plugged into a thousand-watt outlet. All that energy has to go somewhere, so Matt has transformed his environment into a giant drum set."

When Matt drums, regardless of what he is drumming on, he makes music! Check out several videos of him playing drums, a chair, stairs, a bike rack, and other things that a person would never suspect could be used to make music on YouTube or his website, www.drumechoes.com.

Ruth Cahn

Ruth is an amazing woman! She is an extraordinarily talented percussionist, has an insatiable appetite for teaching and is an incredibly kind and patient person. If I had been able to choose the perfect teacher for my son, it would have been Ruth. To see her and then to speak with her, you are captivated by her obvious elegance and gentle, warm and accepting personality. The combination of exceptional talent coupled with amazing teaching abilities in a person who is also nurturing and accepting is unique—and it is Ruth.

I remember sitting outside the practice rooms at the Eastman School of Music during Matthew's lessons. I suddenly heard tics that for many teachers would have been unacceptable. Ruth waited until his tics were done and then continued with the lesson. She recently told me over lunch that she knew nothing about Tourette until meeting Matthew. She credited all the written material I provided her as the reason she learned about Tourette and understood his symptoms.

Ruth once told me that many people can play musical instruments but it is a rare few who, when in front of an audience, make music. She said that Matthew is one of those rare few.

Thank you, Ruth, for teaching my son the mechanics of drumming, a love for music, and most importantly skills that contributed to making him the man he is today.

- 9 -

THE IMPORTANCE OF BALANCE FOR PARENTS

The other side of balance, which was extremely important for everyone in our family, was *my* balance. When Matthew began Kindergarten, the only activity I had been involved in during the past 12 years was volunteering for the Discover Conesus newspaper. This involved reporting on the monthly town board meetings and assisting in putting the paper together once a month. While this was critical for my mental health, I needed more. One day I was cleaning out old college papers and read one that I wrote on Chaucer. I was shocked when I realized that I was having a difficult time understanding it. I knew it wasn't because it was such a scholarly piece of literature! I realized my brain had gotten lazy over the past 12 years.

Working outside the home became a necessity for me. I desperately needed an interest separate from anything to do with Tourette and the house. I required some sort of work in which I felt a level of competency. This was during a time when many people in my life didn't keep it a secret that they believed any difficulties Matthew was experiencing were due to my parenting skills—or lack thereof. I often seriously wondered whether the world was correct and I was totally incompetent as a mother.

I picked up the Penny Saver newspaper that lists cars for sale, used furniture and local employment opportunities. It fell open to the want ad section and there was one that caught my attention immediately. The ad was for an Assistant Director for the Foster Grandparent Program. The job was only 30 minutes away, was part-time and included time off during school holidays.

I had no clue what a Foster Grandparent did. From the ad, I had the impression that it was overseeing senior citizens who worked in schools as a 'grandparent' to help children who needed extra attention. Since I had a background in education, this sounded perfect.

I interviewed for the position on Wednesday, was hired on Friday and began working on Monday. I was excited yet nervous about working in the outside world again. But I thought, "what the heck—I would only be an assistant." Someone else would be telling me what to do and I'm a pretty good worker-bee. How hard could this be?

Monday was a good day. I met with the staff of the agency that managed this program and was given written materials to provide me a better sense of what a foster grandparent did. I met the Director of the Foster Grandparent Program and was relieved to find that she was very nice while also highly motivated and organized. I thought we would work very well together.

Tuesday morning, I arrived before anyone else. I sat at my new desk, reading some brochures that I would use to recruit people to be foster grandparents when I was called to the main building. I was told that the Director of the Foster Grandparent Program was not returning. I was now the Interim Director. They casually added that the following Wednesday was the monthly training day, at which there would be over 60 foster grandparents...and I was in charge. YIKES!

To make a long story short, our secretary, Cleo, knew everything that I needed to do and helped me through those first few months. Thank you, Cleo!

Besides providing an outside interest and the flexibility that allowed me to be home when my kids were not in school, this ended up to be the perfect job for me at that time in my life. First, while my home life often didn't even slightly resemble an environment over which I had control, this job turned out to be something I was not only good at, but also gave me a sense of doing something worthwhile.

But the primary reason this job was perfect was that it involved over 60 grandparent-type people who loved me! They gave me hugs whenever I needed them, and told me what a wonderful person and mother I was. It was like having 60 loving and nurturing grandparents of my own. It's really hard to beat the love and confidence of a grandmother to get past any feelings of inadequacies.

After I had been with the Foster Grandparents Program for a few years, I decided to mix things up at the next monthly meeting. Everyone always sat next to the same person. I wanted them to get to know more than just the few people at their regular tables. So as they entered the building, I handed them a folded piece of paper on which I had written a number. I began the meeting by telling them that I had numbers on the back of every chair and asked them to sit in the chair that had that same number.

I don't know if you can picture the mass confusion that ensued. Imagine sixty senior citizens milling around trying to locate *their* chair. Eighty year old Eva sat with her arms folded and said with conviction, "I have sat in this chair for the last 18 years and I'm not changing now!" The entire spectacle resulted in my laughing so hard that I had tears rolling down my cheeks.

Suddenly, it was as if someone hit me over the head—I was *laughing.* It was the first time in four years I experienced real laughing. Four years without laughter—that's how desperate I was for balance!

I stayed in that position for over eight years, fluctuating between Assistant Director and Interim Director as directors came and went. It really was perfect. The hours were flexible, I had all of the school vacations, and worked with the most wonderful, giving people who loved the children they helped support ...and the *major* bonus, they all loved me! Well,— nothing can be *really* perfect—the pay was pathetic, but the benefits from having grandparents far outweighed the low salary.

It was about this same time that I discovered the joys and benefits of gardening. I would walk out to the garden and just sit quietly soaking in the peace and beauty. But if I didn't like where a plant was located or how it looked, I either moved it to another location or removed it totally. It was my kingdom over which I reigned supreme. Sorry, plant—you're not working for me—off with your head. It was very therapeutic.

I continue to look for what may bring me some balance to my life. The ultimate influences to my balance entered my world November 2009 with the birth of my grandson, Alessio, and May 2012 when my granddaughter, Sofia, was born. They have a way of making all my troubles fade into the background and providing a joyful balance to my life.

Finding balance for Matthew, my marriage, my family and for me was not easy, but it was critical. I wish I could say that I figured this out on my own but it's not true. Events, jobs and people came into our lives and it just happened. It's uncanny how often events that are life-altering occur without recognition of their importance in the moment. What I now identify as essential factors in parenting Matthew actually fell into our laps unexpectedly and without any effort on our part. I am extremely grateful, however!

Colleen Brown

Colleen recognized the importance of balance for Matthew and had a major impact on his career as a keynote presenter. Colleen is the Public Education Coordinator and my co-worker at The Advocacy Center. With amazing efficiency, she does a tremendous job developing disability awareness opportunities in the community and then locating a presenter to fill the need. She helped Matthew when he first began his business, Drum Echoes, Inc., by encouraging his quick wit, excellent communication skills, and dynamic personality while presenting to audiences of all ages.

She initiated numerous school assemblies at which Matt provided disability awareness and bullying prevention presentations to the students and staff. When she didn't co-present, she called the person in charge of the assembly to ensure that he would have plenty of water available during his presentation. She also suggested that they encourage him to begin with a percussion performance. She knew that this not only immediately captivated the audience, it also relaxed Matt. She recognized the importance of these for his balance. Once again, an incredible person came into our lives, providing Matthew precisely what he needed as he began his career.

Thanks, Colleen, for believing in my son. You helped him recognize strategies and reinforced his confidence that he had the necessary skills to have a positive and lasting impact on children and educating professionals regarding the importance of positive supports for all children. Also, thanks for helping me keep *my* balance by going with me every morning before work for coffee, a donut and our often much needed conversations.

- 10 -

DESPERATE TO FIND THE ANSWER

Many times after Matthew finally fell to sleep, I knelt next to his bed and placed my hands on either side of his head, as if I could somehow draw out and heal the symptoms that were responsible for his personal hell. I thought of all the medicines we were putting into his body that were impacting my little boy's brain and prayed that we were doing right by him.

I needed to find The Answer that would allow my son to remain the happy little boy who delighted in life, music, flowers, frogs, dogs, cats, lightening bugs, and butterflies. I needed *The Answer* that would put an end to his being taken over by whatever it was that transformed him into another person that none of us recognized as being the same little boy. I was desperate to find *The Answer* so he could live with his family, play with his brother and sister, go for walks in the woods, and explore the world of nature that he loved so much.

When Matthew was five and first began to have challenging behaviors, I kept journals of everything he ate, what he wore, where he went, laundry detergent, face soap, toothpaste - pretty much everything I could think of in my desperate search to find *something* that might shed a light on how to help him. I felt a sense of overwhelming urgency to find something that would end the torture he experienced. One day as I was dissecting my journal entries looking for a clue, I saw it! I saw *The Answer*! It was Orange Juice—that was it! My notes were clear. When he had orange juice, his symptoms increased dramatically. The days when he didn't drink orange juice, his symptoms were quieter.

So, we removed orange juice from his diet. I had done it; I

had found *The Answer*. My determination to find a way to make his symptoms meaningless in our lives had finally paid off.

Two days later, the meaning of *waxing and waning* was driven home like a stake into my heart. The rage and the symptoms returned. Orange juice was not *The Answer*.

I was exhausting myself. Not only from the amount of time I was dedicating, but also from the emotional disappointment that reoccurred every time I turned over yet another new stone that was useless.

It didn't stop me, though. I continued to be committed to finding *The Answer* that was going to eliminate these symptoms for my son and for our family. I *was* going to find *The Answer*, despite all of my friends, family and professionals who urged me to give it up. I insisted that there *must* be an Answer and by God I was going to find it!

It became obvious to my therapist, Amy, that this search was beginning to consume me and interfere with my life as well as my family's. I will never forget one particular meeting with her. I was relating my latest theory and how this time it was *The Answer* that would help my son. She looked me dead center in my eyes and asked, "What if there is no answer?"

What!?! There *had* to be an answer! How could she be saying this blasphemy?

"What if there is no answer and this is just the way it is?"

My reaction was anger. *Of Course* there was an answer; I just needed to find it. There *had* to be an answer! Matthew hated the rages. It wasn't as if he was an angry person and enjoyed saying mean things to people he loved.

He was loving, funny, bright and a joy to be with the majority of the time. I clung to this, and to the fact that he was always sincerely sorry for what he had done or said. So, there *must* be an answer for those awful out-of-control times. We were good people. Matthew and my other children were wonderful kids. All I needed to do was to figure out how to help him so he didn't lose himself during those times when his brain chemistry was out of balance. I needed to find *The Answer* that would make my son *normal* and my family *normal* again.

Some professionals working with us thought they might have the answer. They encouraged us to use the strategies that had worked for other families with more *typical* difficulties. They assumed that they would work for us as well. Everyone wanted to 'fix' us. I think too often, people who are human service providers feel inadequate if they can't suggest something that helps to 'fix' either the child or the parents. It seemed that people thought there was a simple solution and, for some reason, we hadn't thought of it and no one had suggested it to us. Either that or we weren't really following their suggestions, or at best weren't doing it consistently.

We had numerous counselors, therapists and social workers over the years. Some of them were helpful; others tried to be helpful but we walked away feeling blamed and more tired.

When Matthew was in residential placement, we were required to meet with the social worker every Tuesday afternoon. Tony and I talked with her about the weekend, which typically involved dangerous behaviors, remorse and sadness.

After our discussion, she contacted the cottage where Matthew lived so he could join us. Every week for nine months, this social worker looked at my nine year old son and asked him the same question, "So Matthew, what precipitated the incident? Was your Mom mad at your Dad? Was your Dad mad at your Mom? What precipitated the incident?"

It was these types of questions that almost put me over the edge of sanity. I wanted to shake her by the shoulders and scream "NOTHING PRECIPITATED THE INCIDENT! I ASKED HIM TO PICK UP HIS SOCKS—THAT'S WHAT *PRECIPITATED* THE #@$%&#$ INCIDENT!!!"

But, if I had done that, she would have thought, "Ha! Finally I've discovered the truth!" She would have wrongly assumed that she had identified the real problem. Just as everyone suspected, it *was* bad parenting and one wacky mother!

We periodically had meetings with his entire team. The psychologists, recreation therapists, behavioral therapists, counselors, social workers, and teachers met with Matthew, Tony and me. Everyone had pads of paper on which they took notes. Once again they were scrutinizing the home situation in another attempt to ascertain the reason for Matthew's behaviors and why they only occurred at home.

At one of these meetings, a doctor asked our son, "So, Matthew, what's the worst thing you can think of that your Mom could do to your Dad?" Matthew thought for a moment and said, "Kill him." Everyone began writing furiously on their pads. Someone else asked him, "So, you're afraid that your Mom will kill your Dad?"

Matthew looked shocked and said, "No, but you asked me what's the *worst* thing I can think of and that's the *worst*." Another person then asked, "Okay, knowing your Mom, what's the worst thing you think she would do to your Dad?"

Again, Matthew thought for a minute and said, "Probably throw a pillow at him."

Phew! I hate to think what would have occurred if that second person had not asked him a follow-up question. It's really unfortunate that so many therapists and counselors who mean well say things they believe will be helpful, but instead result in (again) blaming the parents.

When Matthew was 11, an agency that was providing us support offered to pay all expenses for Tony and me to attend a mental health conference in Albany, NY. The date fell on our wedding anniversary. Fantastic! We were excited to be able to get away for a weekend that we couldn't have afforded otherwise. It was a bonus that we were able to attend a conference that would provide us with information that would help us with parenting our son. Maybe it was here that I would find *The Answer*.

One of the sessions was titled "The Neurochemistry of Aggressive Children." This was definitely a lecture I wanted to attend. As we entered the room and saw the presenter, we both noticed that he was very young. I suspected that he didn't have a great deal of real life experience under his belt. But, he had excellent credentials so I tried not to make assumptions. Instead my expectations were that I would learn from him how my son's brain functioned. I was confident that this information would get me closer to *The Answer*.

Back in the day, colored name tags were given to attendees of conferences designating them as either a parent or a professional. Red was the color for parents at this conference. I noticed that the majority of people in the room wore red name tags.

The presenter began by telling us that he was the lead researcher on a project exploring the home life of children with behavioral issues. He explained that the study involved three families with young children who were all in elementary school and had aggressive behaviors. I thought three families wasn't exactly an extensive study, but again I tried to keep an open mind and listen to what the results of the research were.

The children were all found to have low levels of a specific neurotransmitter called serotonin. I had never heard that term at the time, but he explained that low levels of this particular chemical greatly increased the likelihood of violent behaviors in animal studies. It was also well documented that *stress* was responsible for the reduction of this important neurotransmitter.

Members of the study team visited with each family for a week, noting in particular the interactions between the mother and the child. Their reports all indicated that the mothers were consistently less loving, less nurturing and interacted much less with the child who was aggressive. They reported that these mothers had less positive verbal and physical interaction with the child than was the norm.

The doctor told the audience—made up primarily of mothers—that after a great deal of study, their findings were that the reason the children were aggressive was due to a reduction in serotonin, caused by the extreme stress of a non-caring mother. There was silence from the audience. As I looked around, I saw people silently shaking their heads in agreement. I also saw a lowering of heads and shoulders as if they were now carrying even more weight than when they first walked into the session which they hoped would help their child.

My husband typically prefers to blend into the crowd, so I had promised him that I wouldn't say anything controversial or disagree with any presenters. I tried very hard for a few seconds; then I suddenly realized my hand was in the air.

The presenter called on me. I asked if they had also considered the possibility that these children were born with an abnormally low level of serotonin and *that* might possibly be responsible for these children being aggressive. I took a deep breath and continued. Further, if this is a possibility, could it be true that after years of extremely difficult behaviors, the mothers were exhausted and afraid of any interaction that might set off yet another aggressive episode—*particularly* in front of a stranger who was evaluating her skills as a parent?

He admitted that they had not considered this in their study. Suddenly, some of the same mothers in the audience who had, prior to my questions, looked defeated now had their hands in the air. They related their own stories to back up this possibility.

Just as it is easy to blame the child, it is also easy to blame the parents for their child's difficult behaviors…particularly the mother.

To be honest, when Matthew first began having challenging behaviors, I *wanted* it to be my fault. I wanted one of the professionals we were seeing to say, "I have *The Answer*; this is *your* fault." At the time, I desperately wanted someone to educate me as to specifically what I was doing wrong and how I could change. I wanted *The Answer* to be me. *I could change!* I would do anything! I just needed to know what to do differently. But, no one could say explicitly what I was doing wrong and what to do differently—at least nothing that helped.

I attended another conference; this one was intended for school counselors and school psychologists. When I saw it advertised, I called the phone number that was listed to see if parents could attend. I was told that parents wouldn't be able to comprehend the information presented. Hmmmmmm. I told her nicely that even though I was a parent, I was certified to teach seventh through twelfth grade English and I had studied challenging behaviors for years. She wasn't convinced. I promised her I would sit quietly and not ask any questions. She interrupted and repeated, this time more sternly, that parents could not attend. (Maybe she had been at that conference I attended with my husband and recognized my voice?)

I didn't want to argue with her. I already knew I would attend regardless of what she was saying and didn't want to give her a heads-up that I might sneak in. The day arrived. I dressed in my most convincing school psychologist's outfit and signed in under a school district that was relatively far away, hoping that no one from that school would be there to blow my cover.

When the presenter asked for questions, one of the school psychologists (assuming she wasn't pretending to be one like I was) raised her hand and said that she was working with a young student with Tourette syndrome, and that this youngster displayed aggressive behaviors. She asked him to please comment on this. The doctor said that there were only three reasons why a youngster with Tourette, ADD, OCD, and other diagnoses would display these types of behaviors.

First, many children act out in a desperate attempt to impress other students in order to make friends. Secondly, he said that these children often don't have control over their bodies at any given moment so they become frustrated, angry and therefore act out.

I recognized both of these as possibilities.

The third reason, this doctor said, was because the "mom" needs to be placed on medication.

Everyone laughed, except me. I suppose that this was an attempt at humor! But, I also think that he truly believed this to be true. As the saying goes, "many truths are said in jest."

It took all of my restraint, but I didn't respond. I was afraid that if I had said anything, I would have proven his point. See this "Mom"? She obviously needs to be on medication!

I wanted to leave immediately, but managed to control my urge until the next break. I left frustrated and angry that so many professionals couldn't get past blaming parents.

Once again, I had expected to find *The Answer*. Instead, I witnessed a lack of knowledge from a respected professional who had told this large group of educators who work with youngsters that if all else fails, it's the mother's fault.

To my husband's credit, he never accepted that it was our fault and never doubted our abilities as parents. For too many years, I remained under the misguided belief that it was my fault and, therefore, I would be able to change it. He never bought into that possibility.

But, you know what? It really wasn't my fault! I wanted so desperately to find *The Answer*, that I was even willing to accept the blame. Because of this, I tried strategies that made no sense. I was told that I needed to punish more. So we removed a toy for every 'inappropriate response' until he had no toys left. Most professionals insisted that if we consistently sent him to his room for 'time out' that eventually this behavior would stop. They said that we needed to tell him to stay there until he was told he could come out. They clearly had no concept of life in our house. Apparently they could not conceive of any family situations in which all attempts at *making* our son do what he was opposed to doing almost always failed miserably. I understand that this is an extremely difficult concept for people to accept.

We arrived week after week for our sessions with social workers more and more bruised emotionally and mentally. They showed us methods of restraining him that were *guaranteed* to work; if done correctly, he would not be able to hurt us and it would calm him. But, Matthew would head-butt, bite, spit in our face, kick, whatever was necessary and it lasted for hours, not minutes as they had promised. The restraints, the timeouts, the

punishments; all of the spanking, screaming, threatening…
Nothing…*nothing* worked!

I had no control over my son. How does this make a mother
feel? Surely I was a failure.

During a visit to one of the many therapists that we worked
with over the years, we were told that every time Matthew said or
did something that was "inappropriate," we were to *calmly* tell
him that he would need to spend five minutes in his room. We
had *never* tried "calmly." I'm not making a joke or being
sarcastic; we truly had not tried being calm when he was in a
rage.

Okay, we would try telling him *calmly* that he needed to go
to his room.

I don't think we were even out of the parking lot before
Matthew asked me if I had a needle and thread in my purse. Trust
me, I admire mothers who have purses with an incredible variety
of items that people might need, but that's not me.

I said the word that we would learn should be avoided at all
costs. I said, "No." Matthew immediately replied, "Bitch, why
not?"

Okay…I considered what the doctor said and *calmly* replied,
"That's an inappropriate thing to say so when we get home. You
will need to spend five minutes in your room."

"I'm not going to go to my damn room when I get home."

(Calmly) "That is inappropriate so you have another five
minutes."

"Go to hell, I'm not going to my room."

(Calmly) "That's not appropriate. That is another five
minutes."

"Shut up—I'm not going to my room."

(Calmly) "That also isn't appropriate, so you will need to
spend an additional five minutes."

"Fuck you. I'm not going to my room."

Time in his room rapidly progressed to two and a half hours; Matthew was escalating and my husband turned and said, "I don't think this is working."

But you know, in a way, it *did* work and I learned something very important that day. In the past under the same situation, the ride would have been dangerous. It wasn't this time. I'm not saying it was fun, but it hadn't been one in which my son and I screamed at each other. I actually felt better. I felt calmer and less 'beat up' because I had remained calm throughout. By staying calm, I had maintained control of the situation. I hadn't 'fixed him' or cured him of his neurological disorder—but I had maintained control of *my* emotional response *and* the ride was safe. This was the beginning of the realization that by not getting pulled into the rage and instead remaining calm, I was more in charge of the situation than ever before. I'm not saying it was easy, but as I saw it work to my benefit, it actually did get easier over the years.

We tried all the approaches that people suggested; all the strategies that parents use: stickers, earned points, losing points, written rules posted on the refrigerator, charts for rewards, old fashioned spanking, time out, loss of privileges, incentives of all sorts.

The reason that none of these work in our situation was because Matthew wanted very much to do what was expected of him; he knew right from wrong. The fact remained that he wasn't able to behave in a manner that he both *knew* and *wanted* to behave. He couldn't process disappointments, unexpected changes, frustration, or how to be flexible *in the moment.* He absolutely knew right from wrong, but as he became stressed, the chemicals in his brain were altered, causing faulty mental brakes. We needed to find a different way to parent Matthew.

It took me a while to come to the conclusion that if a professional told me they had *The Answer*, it was almost certain that they didn't. If someone thought that they had *The Answer* to these complex neurological disorders then they weren't looking for clues—and, in my opinion, without being open to all possibilities, they would never find *any* answers.

Why can't people consider that instead of being the parents' and/or the child's fault that there are children with brains that function differently, which results in behavioral differences? That's what it is. Different. Just like a child with insulin imbalance has diverse issues, our child had different issues. That's all. Nothing more, nothing less.

AMY PITT

My position at The Advocacy Center frequently required that I provide presentations regarding different aspects of parenting a child with disabilities. One day, I was presenting to a large group of parents and professionals when a man in the back ask me a question that surprised me. He said, "What I want to know is which drugs do *you* take?" Everyone laughed, but I knew what he was asking. It's actually somewhat common for people to ask me what helped me to remain sane throughout all of this. Easy answer! My therapist, counselor, and teacher, Amy Pitt.

Among the top things that I would recommend to parents who are raising a child with challenging behavior disorders is to find a counselor/therapist who you trust and who doesn't rely on a 'blame and shame' style of therapy.

I saw Amy recently and I asked her why she hadn't tried to give me advice as others always had done. Her response was, "How could I give you advice? I never parented a child similar to Matthew." I asked her if she could tell me what she had done that helped me to survive all those years. She said that she *listened* and she *cared*. She never denied or talked me out of feeling my pain because it was real and needed to be felt, even though I didn't want to. And I *really* didn't want to!

Getting me to feel emotions was one of Amy's challenges working with me. I had shut down my feelings as a protection. I clung to the belief that it was better for me to stand firmly in the middle of the "emotional teeter totter." No ups; no downs. She told me that people can't shut down only one feeling; it's all or nothing. If I remained in the middle of the "emotional teeter totter," it was true that I wouldn't feel the huge and painful downs but I also wouldn't feel the incredible and joyful ups.

I wasn't used to experiencing a person who really listened and focused on *my* well-being. Amy's focus was *me*—not Matthew, not my family; *me*. And by doing that, she was helping Matthew and my family. The work she did with me gave me the strength to continue on and in a manner that was healthy for me and my entire family.

One of my presentations is titled "Baggage." I discuss both positive and not-so-positive pieces of baggage that we carry around as parents. I talk about how they either help us or get in the way of helping our child with difficulties. Our emotional baggage may explode if someone pushes the wrong button. My message for this presentation is that the better we know our own baggage, the better we are at communicating with those people who can help our children. For instance, I am more likely to be able to keep my anger in check if I know precisely what can push my buttons. I am then much better at getting my point across as I advocate for my son.

The presentation involves an old suitcase in which I have many props. Getting through airport security with my 'baggage' is sometimes a daunting experience. I also have items that represent positive experiences. One such item is a sailboat that represents the impact Amy had on my life. During the difficult years, it was as if my sails were ripped to shreds, the wind had been knocked out of me, and I couldn't move forward. I met with Amy and somehow she patched my sails in a manner that allowed me to make it through another week. The following week, she again patched up my sails so that I could navigate another week.

Amy didn't have The Answer to what would make my family normal again. But she did have the answer to what I needed…she cared and she listened. Additionally, she taught me life lessons, with her incredible patience, often a bizarre sense of humor and tremendous wisdom.

I, in no way, am suggesting that meeting with a counselor was easy or fun. At one session I was once again blaming myself. She said, "You continue to blame yourself and say that this is your fault. Would you like to hear my thoughts regarding that?" When I said that I did, she said, "You can't handle it if it's *not your* fault. If it isn't your fault, then you don't have any control over the situation, and you can't change it. You can't handle that." At first I was really angry at what she had said. But like many things she would tell me over the years, she was right. I was terrified to accept that it wasn't my fault! That meant that I couldn't control or change what was occurring.

So the first and most important thing I did to take care of myself was to work, and I do mean *work*, with a therapist. We didn't have extra money for non-essentials; but I also couldn't afford *not* to see her.

Amy knew very little about Tourette when I first walked through her door. She never pretended to know what I needed to do, or what I was doing wrong. She helped me to survive and to continue to be the best parent I knew how to be, even though neither of us had any answers. Instead, she listened, asked questions or made observations that encouraged me to be curious. Being curious was what I really needed to do. Blaming me didn't help anyone. Being curious about how I could support Matthew was most successful.

So even though I said I wasn't going to give advice, if I were asked to, I'd say to find a good therapist, counselor or support person. It's far better to go without something else so that you can pay a good therapist/counselor—someone you trust, someone who cares and listens. I actually would put what Amy did for me in a different way. She *caringly listened.*

I recognize that good counselors are not a 'dime a dozen.' It's important to find the right person. I was incredibly fortunate to find Amy. She kept me sane. She helped my family remain healthy.

Amy, you assured me over 20 years ago that even though you didn't have *The Answer*, you planned to be there for me "for the long haul." Thanks for keeping that promise.

- 11 -

HOPE—THE *OTHER* FOUR LETTER WORD

When Matthew was eight years old, his neurologist requested governmental permission to prescribe Prozac for a youngster. Within two days of beginning this medication, the constant obsessive/compulsive behaviors were quiet. The swearing and screeching that began as soon as Matthew woke up and didn't end until he finally fell asleep—his symptoms were almost gone. We had found *The Answer*! Our wonderful doctor had found the miracle medication that allowed my family to once again be *normal*. HOPE! HOPE!! HOPE!!!

We laughed more, ate dinner together, all rode in one car, visited neighbors and family. HOPE! Hope that my son's nightmare was over.

Then came the day it ended. It was almost as if his brain recognized that it had been fooled by messing around with its chemistry and had re-adjusted back to the way it was before Prozac.

Our lives crashed back to reality. Matthew woke up screaming and immediately threw and broke one of the knickknacks I mistakenly assumed was safe to take out of the box hidden under my bed. My son was once again trapped in the world of symptoms. Back to the reality which, at the time, seemed to be ours alone. I had my first experience with the pain that can result when false hopes are dashed against the rocks of reality.

Matthew's vocal tics included the 'four letter word' that people think of first. I was beginning to hear from everyone around me another word that became my personal 'four letter word'…Hope.

"You always have to have hope."

"We can never give up on hope."

"Hope is precious."

"Hopefully next year will be better."

"You need to hope for the best."

"If you don't have hope, you don't have anything."

I believe there should be two different words for the concept of 'hope.' One would represent the immediate and false hope that this new medication was *the answer*; hope that we had found the cure. The other would be a long term hope—the Hope that his life will improve as he becomes an adult; Hope that he will have a happy and productive life.

How do I explain to people who don't have a child with these difficulties that for *some* parents, there are times when the here-and-now-false hope can result in very real and reoccurring pain? There were hundreds of times that I hoped and believed the '*bad times*' were behind us. This hope may have been a result of a brief period when symptoms were reduced due to a new medication, or the waxing and waning of symptoms so common with these complex disorders.

When Matthew was young, there were years I felt it was almost better to have consistent difficulties instead of brief moments of *normalcy*. I know that sounds strange, but when we would have a good week or even a good day, the flame of hope would, without hesitance, ignite in the depth of my heart. I was never very good at being cautious at recognizing it was only a *possibility* that this moment would continue and become a lasting reality. Instead, any small reason for hope would burst inside me with an all-consuming flame.

I immediately clung to the hope that his symptoms were now, and would forever be, GONE…finally, our delightful son was back…to stay. I had hope that he would not be over taken ever again by symptoms which were so distressing to everyone. I felt hope that we could now lead a *normal* life. That we could have dinner together and do things as a family; even go to the movies on the spur of the moment.

But our world always crashed again! Symptoms came back, sometimes worse than they had been before our brief 'vacation' on this false island of hope. I wasn't able to be cautious of hope. I was never able to say to myself—"this is how it is right now. Enjoy the moment."

"Hope springs eternal." Yes, it does.

When there was a good day, a day of laughter, hugs and *typical* family interactions, resisting the pull of hope was fruitless. Hope rose to the surface at the smallest sign that my little boy had returned; hope was back and I reveled in it.

No matter how many times I told myself to be cautious; don't count on this good time lasting very long, I would instead consistently grasp onto the hope that this time would be different—this time there was good reason to hope.

Riding the fast ups and the crashing downs was excruciating. Putting one foot in front of the other, numbing my responses to the ups and downs was somehow better than experiencing the pain that came in the wake of crashing hope. I worked at turning off my feelings; it was less painful that way. My therapist attempted to have me recognize the reality of the moment instead of riding the roller coaster called hope. The reality was that today was good, tomorrow may be good…or not.

This in *No Way* is intended to imply that I didn't have the deep-inside-my-being Hope and belief in Matthew as a child, as a person, or for his future. If I learned anything from this journey, I am convinced of the importance of parents believing in their child's abilities and goodness and validating these at every opportunity. I committed myself to making sure that Erika, Jeff and Matthew recognized my absolute confidence in their integrity, in their abilities, and their futures as productive adults.

Despite Matthew's severe symptoms, I saw his potential even when he was young. Have I ever stopped being hopeful for his future? Absolutely NOT! I never stopped believing in

Matthew! It was the hope of a *cure* that I needed to let go of; the hope that he would never again have symptoms. The hope that my incredible son who gave me so much joy would no longer have symptoms that got in his way of being who he was and longed to be.

Liz Greenberg, a good friend and insightful woman, helped me with editing this book. In conversation with her about the pain caused by the concept of hope, I could tell that she really wasn't buying into what I was saying. I told her that I struggled with this chapter and whether to include it because I wasn't sure I could clearly express my thoughts on this in a way that would make sense—even to other parents who were living a similar life.

I asked her if she had ever seen the movie "Awakenings" starring Robin Williams. She had, and we talked about how deeply it had affected us both. She told me she cried through the entire last half. I'd like to share with you my experience of watching this film and how it may help to better explain my struggles with this thorny concept of hope.

One evening, during the time that Matthew was not able to live at home, Tony and I saw that a movie titled "Awakenings" was going to be on TV. Since it starred Robin Williams, we assumed that it was a comedy. We certainly could use some light entertainment and looked forward to spending a couple of hours watching something that might allow us to laugh and not think about disabilities or symptoms of neurological disorders.

How wrong we were!

"Awakenings" is a movie about the real-life Dr. Oliver Sacks. In his early years as a physician, he worked with patients who were catatonic after surviving the early 1900s epidemic of encephalitis. There was a conversation amongst the physicians regarding patients who were unable to speak and were significantly limited in movements. They talked about these people being stuck in a "tic-like symptom." I heard that phrase and my ears perked up.

Everyone believed that there was nothing that could be done to help them, *except* Dr. Sacks, who was persistent in his efforts at finding a cure. One of these treatments was a new drug that impacted dopamine levels in the brain.

Wait! Did they say dopamine? The first medication Matthew had been placed on was Haldol, which impacts dopamine in the brain. Clearly this wasn't a comedy, but I no longer cared because my interest had been piqued. I heard words that were used by our doctors and words that I had read about in the books I was devouring in my search to find *The Answer*.

In the movie when the patients were given this new drug, they suddenly came back to life—they *awakened* and their symptoms were gone. They danced; they ate; they went out to restaurants and to movies; they began to explore and discover the world that had left them behind.

The joy I felt was unfathomable; impossible to describe. I wanted to scream from the rooftop, "See...there IS an ANSWER!"

Everyone had told Dr. Sacks to just accept and to stop looking for an answer, just as people were telling me. But instead, he kept looking and, lo and behold, he had found *The Answer!* I couldn't wait to call my doctor and talk about using Haldol again—there must be a better type than the kind we had tried just a couple of years ago. It was *The Answer*. HOPE! My entire world was engulfed in an inferno of hope.

The movie continued, however. The medication lost its effectiveness. The patients went back to being 'stuck.' They returned to the way they had been before taking Haldol. Dr. Sacks, of course, kept experimenting, trying desperately to bring them back to life again. But the brain is very complex. It had been fooled for a moment by this medicine, but returned to being stuck. The people never found their way to being 'un-stuck' again.

I was devastated. I cried from the depth of my being. Maybe, indeed, there was no answer...Maybe there was no reason to hope, and that hope only brings pain.

I eventually learned that my thoughts regarding 'hope' were what I *wanted* to be true and not what *was* true.

At long last, I no longer hope that he is cured. (Well, between you and me, I guess there is a tiny bit of me that hangs onto that.) But it doesn't jerk me around anymore from the deep lows to the false highs that I felt when Matthew was younger. I got off that ride and now try very hard to take every day as being what it is—not what I want it to be. I live in the here and now rather than in a future that relies on hoping for that elusive cure.

By the way, just so you know, I have *never* enjoyed riding roller coasters—even as a child!

DENISE BUSCEMI

I met Denise at Partners in Policy Making, a training program for individuals and parents of children with disabilities. She was there because of her beautiful daughter, Nylah, who had spinal bifida. This group met one weekend a month for an eight-month period. The weekend was filled with lectures, activities and opportunities to connect with other family members and people with disabilities. The training changed my life as a parent, as a person, and as a professional. It provided me with a confidence that I never dreamed I would have. It drastically altered my ability to advocate for my son, my future career, and my work with families.

Another positive outcome of this training was developing a friendship with Denise. She is more than 12 years my junior, but that has no impact on our friendship—well maybe a little because it provides fodder for some teasing on both sides. She has had a remarkable life filled with far too many challenges and difficult times, but she continues to put one foot in front of the other with remarkable grace.

The one advantage of having a child with a disability is that you have an automatic membership in a very exclusive 'club' that demands a major shift in life priorities. Denise and I have been friends for many years and have been there for each other through it all.

When I'm with Denise, the environment is one of honesty, because there really is no other way; we have nothing to hide from each other. We know each other in a way that can be achieved only by spending hours upon hours sharing the good and the difficult. It's about having each other's back and a deep understanding of each other's lives.

As I write this, Denise is with her 12 year old son in another state, far away from her other children. He is facing major health issues that she has already experienced with her older son. We both understand her exhaustion and thoughts that she just can't do this again. And we both know that she doesn't have a choice. She will get through whatever the future holds. And she will do it with *grace*, because that is Denise. I have seen this when she has faced other struggles. I have experienced it when she has helped me with my struggles.

I understand when people tell me that they don't want to be with other parents of children with disabilities because it is too depressing. But don't allow these times to prevent you from seeking out parents of children with difficulties.

There is a saying that your friends are family members that you get to choose. Keep looking for those people who can be your chosen family. Denise is like a sister to me, as are some of my other friends who have children with differences. They are critical to my having the strength to move forward during hard times and allow me to laugh and joke as only people who are in the 'club' can understand.

Don't deny yourself this—it's actually an amazing benefit, exclusively for those who belong to that club none of us would have chosen to join in the first place. If I hadn't had the necessary qualifications to join (that is, Matthew) I would have missed out on an opportunity to get to know Denise and so many others who I am so, so honored to call my friends and co-workers.

Denise gave me a beautiful dove-like pin during a time when my life was particularly difficult. It doesn't represent the hope that Matthew will someday be cured, but rather the buoyancy that no matter what happens, I have friends who love me regardless of what craziness I throw their way.

- 12 -

A Quest for Companions on the Journey

As I smashed a broom against the basement wall again and again, I turned and looked up the stairs to see all three of my children looking down at me. It really wasn't hard to read their minds. They all had looks on their faces that said, "What is Mom doing and should we run and hide?"

Thankfully, we lived way out in the country. Nobody could hear when either one or all of us 'lost it.' I know of too many families who have been reported to child protective services because neighbors heard the sound of yelling and items being broken, and made the assumption that the child was being abused. In reality it is often a parent trying to do the best they can under extreme circumstances for which no one, or no past experiences had prepared them.

Just in case you might think that I did this parenting thing really well, I want you to know that I did the best I could *in that moment.* That's all any of us can do. There were so many times when a survival instinct lead me to consider getting in the car and heading in any direction that would take me far away. Not great mothering, but I had to also accept that I was definitely not super human. I was far from perfect and sometimes just too exhausted.

We tried parenting in the way we considered as *normal*, or at least sort of normal. But when the techniques that worked on our other children didn't work for Matthew, we became desperate to bring some normalcy to the family. But, there wasn't anyone to talk with; no internet to explore for techniques, no families that had lived through a similar experience and the advice from professionals most often fell short.

I'm not proud of many of the things I did. It took way to long for me to come to the realization that I needed to parent Matthew in a very different way than my other two children, and differently than I had seen, heard of or read about anywhere! For far too long, I continued to use the typical parenting strategies even though they continued not to work.

No one was around when I, with the urging of a professional, put soap in my four year old boy's mouth because he repeatedly called me a jerk. I put soap in his mouth consistently, because that's what we have learned works to extinguish a negative behavior—consistent punishment. Every time he called me a jerk, out came the soap. He would run from me covering his mouth, begging me not do this. But I had been assured by a professional counselor that this type of punishment, when used *consistently,* would break him of this behavior! So I did it.

One day after he had begged me not to do it, I put soap in my mouth just to see what it was like. It's child abuse. My only excuse is that this was prior to his diagnosis and behaviors were heading in a direction that scared the hell out of me. I was desperate.

No one saw me lock him in his room with a metal rod, which was the only way we could keep him from breaking through a closed door. Memories of those times are hard for me. I still experience the shame and huge sadness for having done this to my little boy.

But I learned that self-blame doesn't really help anyone. My therapist asked me once when I was beating myself up, to consider what I would say to another parent if they told me these difficult stories. It was much easier to see that I would remind them they are only human, and that these were enormously difficult years that just seemed to have no end.

I just didn't have a clue how to parent my little boy, and the only way I knew to discipline was with punishment. I wish that we'd had a diagnosis when he was much younger and that I knew punishment would never work. I wish I had known that I needed to work harder and be more creative at determining how I could help him instead of listening to advice from other people who also didn't have a clue.

Yep, I really did some things that now sound ridiculous. Once I threw a souvenir pen out of the car window as we drove home from visiting my sister in North Carolina. Matthew was being "unacceptable" so I did what parents do. I threatened him with the old line, "THAT'S IT! If you do that again you will regret it." He did it; so out the window with the prized pen. The thing is, as I look back, I don't even remember what he did that struck me as being totally unacceptable. But boy, I showed him!…Yeah, right.

Nobody was with us one night when I was helping him get ready for bed. It had been a very long day filled with 'Fuck you,' 'Fuck you,' 'Fuck you, Mom,' 'Fuck you,' and on and on and on. By now I knew very well that this was a symptom of his Tourette syndrome. But, you know, there just are those times when you are so tired it takes only one more thing to put you over the edge. This was one of those moments. Hearing one last 'Fuck you, Mom,' put me over. I turned to my eight year old and said, "Fuck you too, Matthew."…Sigh…

He looked at me, covered his mouth with both his hands, sucked in his breath, eyes wide with shock, and said, "*You* don't say that word. That's a bad word. I'm going to tell my doctor what you said!" My only thought was, "Great, this will only convince *everyone* what they already suspect—my son's problems really *are* because of a lousy mother." Damn…

The list goes on and on with examples of things I did when I was angry and acted in ways of which I am not proud. But I had to learn to accept that I made mistakes and will make more. I was right, I still do.

This all began in the late 1980s and I read everything I could find that was written about Tourette syndrome. This was precisely one book that was 1,200 pages long. A few years back,

I was speaking to college students about disorders and what we had learned from our life. One of them asked why I didn't look for information on the internet. Ahhh, life before the internet and Google.

I began reading books as they became available and asked questions of professionals. I took in what made sense to me and dismissed what didn't. There was a lot of advice that didn't feel right. I would make every attempt at considering it in a detached sort of way, as much as I could. Then if it still didn't fit, I'd file it into my "they just don't know what they are talking about" file and pretty much ignored the advice.

As the years went on, I learned more about how the brain works than I ever thought I would want to know. One thing became more and more clear as I did research: my son's difficulties were due to chemical imbalances, not bad parenting and not because he was a bad person. He was not a bad child who needed increased punishment. He was a good kid whose eyes sparkled when he discovered something new to explore and asked endless questions about how it worked. He was my little boy, who told me every day how much he loved me and what a wonderful mom I was.

I was desperate to find someone who could give me *any* information or firsthand experience because I believed that with enough information, I would find *The Answer* to help my son and my family. I went to all the conferences I could find which even remotely related to our experience. In 1991, I drove to a nearby city to attend my first Tourette syndrome conference.

I was beside myself with excitement and anticipation. Finally I would be with parents who had a child whose behaviors were similar to my son's. It was even possible that there would be parents of *older* children who were now successful adults. They would be able to tell me how to help my son, my other children, my husband, my marriage and myself.

At the very least, I would meet parents of children with unusual symptoms; maybe not as severe as Matthew's, but possibly in the same ball park. I would hear professionals talk about these difficult and dangerous symptoms and gain some much needed guidance on how to raise a child diagnosed with severe Tourette syndrome and challenging behaviors. Best of all, I would no longer be alone. I would be meeting parents who would understand because they were living lives comparable to ours.

When I arrived, I walked toward a large group engrossed in discussion. I overhead them talking about the constant clearing of throats, sniffing, shrugging shoulders, tapping, and blinking eyes. They were comparing stories and talking about how these tics drove them crazy—but I heard nothing about rage or violence. I decided to wander around and eavesdrop on other groups. I was certain that I would be able to locate the group where I belonged and where I would fit in.

As I moved from conversation to conversation, no one was talking about kitchen chairs being slammed over and over until they broke. No one was talking about screeching for hours, kicking holes in walls so large that there was little left of the wall. No stories about lying on the floor spinning in circles and swearing for over two hours; no out-of-control meltdowns that would last three to four hours; no confessions about needing to lock their child in his room because of behaviors that were so dangerous.

I have learned over the years that we really can't compare life experiences. Difficult is difficult! Pain is pain. There is no yardstick to demonstrate that my sadness is worse than any other person's. Sad is sad. But it was challenging on that day to hear people talk and stop myself from thinking that my family's life was more difficult.

It wasn't the people who attended the conference who were to blame for my not finding kindred spirits. They belonged there and needed information and support. No it wasn't them—it was *me*. I was desperate to hear about the dangerous behaviors and symptoms that resulted in the Dr. Jekyll and Mr. Hyde atmosphere that consumed our home. I needed to hear about the symptoms that resulted in the destruction of prized possessions;

of behaviors that were dangerous. I desperately and selfishly wanted to hear of other children who were convinced that God hated them and wanted to die because they were so 'bad.'

By the time I walked into the room where the presentation would take place, I was discouraged and convinced that it was possible I wouldn't meet anyone who could be a companion in this journey. I was, however, certain that the professionals would talk about why my son could be calm one minute and suddenly turn into a child who had anger and violence that no amount of punishment could control or change. I had little doubt that the speakers would give me the advice that would teach me how to make my family normal again.

I was wrong. They spoke to the issues that the other parents were discussing, but nothing was said about what I wanted to hear.

By the time I left at the end of the day, I was devastated. I had gone to this conference expecting to leave with answers and no longer feeling the despair of isolation. Instead what I had found was the opposite. What I left with was that my son *was* the only child in the world who had symptoms that resulted in violence and aggression; that what so many people were telling me *was* true—Matthew's difficulties were actually a result of my poor parenting.

Fortunately, soon after that Tony and I met Mary.

MARY KLEHR

We attended a support group meeting for parents of children with Tourette syndrome held at a couple's house. We were asked to take turns introducing ourselves; Mary began.

She said that most days she was exhausted just attempting to get through breakfast. She told us that every morning as she poured the milk onto her son's cereal, he needed to wave his spoon over the cereal three times *before* the milk hit the cereal. *If* the milk hit the cereal first, she needed to throw the cereal away and start all over with new cereal and new milk. This would only end when her son completed the three swipes of the spoon before the milk hit the cereal. If it happened quickly, there was a chance that it would be a good day for both of them. But it usually wasn't.

Oh My God! I WAS NOT ALONE. We had the exact same ritual occurring at our house in the morning, with the cereal, with the milk, with the spoon AND with the three swipes before the milk hit the cereal! There was someone else in the world that had a similar life as mine!

Mary and I bonded immediately. We spent the next 12 years supporting each other in various ways. We were each other's life line to sanity. We were no longer alone!

Soon after our first meeting, Mary, her husband, my husband and I became members of the "severe support group."

- 1 3 -

THE "SEVERE SUPPORT GROUP"

Would I be interested in meeting other parents living with similar situations? The social worker that worked with Matthew's pediatric neurologist asked me this question, which ultimately changed my life. My answer was, "Would I EVER!"

This particular pediatric group was the only one within 200 miles that specialized in neuro-behavior disorders. Therefore, Joan, the social worker, was in a unique position of having access to the five families who all thought they were the only ones in the world who had a child affected significantly by Tourette syndrome, other neurological disorders and challenging behaviors.

I will never know exactly why Joan decided to bring families like us together. It doesn't matter; we would never have found each other without her. We shared a common story—not exactly the same, but similar enough. And because of that, we met once a month for the next seven years. The same people—some as couples, some not—met monthly for seven years! That is an amazing statistic for any support group. No one dropped out and no one new joined us.

About three years after the group first met, Joan asked a new family to attend. It only took one meeting for them to be too terrified to return. You could see it on their faces as we shared stories about the past month's escapades. They looked at each other with panic while the rest of us laughed so hard that tears ran down our cheeks. I don't think their situation was similar enough for them to be able to garner any support from us. Instead we terrified them. That was why we called it the "severe support group." Joan never invited another family to attend one of our meetings.

A few students from a graduate level social work program at the university and hospital where we met each month asked if they could research our group for their year-end project. Word of the longevity of our group had gotten around, and people wanted to know why we all regularly and for so many years attended these support meetings. The reason really was quite simple; it was the only place in the world where we could talk honestly about our lives without the fear of being judged or perceived to be bad parents. When I say that it was the only place, I really mean—the *only* place. We could share stories and feelings that other people would never understand.... but this group *did*. There were never any hints at being judged; there was only acceptance, mutual respect and support.

For me, one of the most helpful aspects was to meet other parents who were good, decent, loving people and had children with behaviors that were at times dangerous. This allowed me to more easily recognize and accept that since I didn't see *their* child's difficulties as being *their* fault, there was a strong possibility that *my* child's symptoms weren't my fault either. Since *they* were good people, there was the possibility that I was as well—regardless of what people 'outside the club' may have believed.

These parents were your regular, run-of-the-mill 'normal' parents who loved their children. They were good parents who were as lost, confused and devastated as my husband and I.

We were able to share strategies, stories and ways to cope, however, no one pretended to have The Answers. Clearly there weren't any. Not one of us ever hinted that our situation was better or worse than anyone else's. We were all experiencing similar lives. But we had each other. We weren't alone anymore!

I now know that there are actually a lot of parents with similar experiences. It's important that we keep reminding ourselves that we are parents of kids whose brain chemistry makes them do things they don't want to do. We are their parents who love them and do the best job we know how to do. They are children doing the best job they are capable of doing. It just happens to be *different* than what we expected and different from what most of the rest of the world expects.

Parents often fear that a support group will only focus on negative aspects and they will leave the meeting more depressed than before. Joan would not have allowed unnecessary and on-going anger in this group—it wasn't why we met. They weren't bitch sessions or pity parties. It was a support group.

Attending monthly meetings with people in this group was a major reason why our family made it through those hard years. We had a friendship and closeness that was beyond any other; we actually became a family, of sorts. We shared our grief, our exhaustion, frustration, tears, joys and even laughter, similar to a family. The stories that we shared would make others outside our group speechless, but we were able to laugh at each other's incredible situations—similar to the way families can laugh at shared experiences. It was usually the only time I laughed all month.

I remember Mary telling us about her frustration from having to regularly replace the refrigerator door because her son had a compulsion to slam it over and over until it 'felt right.' One day as he was slamming it, Mary went into the garage and began to slam his bike against the wall. Her son ran out and asked what the hell she was doing. She told him that from now on, every time he slammed the refrigerator, she would slam his bike. It didn't prevent him from needing to slam the door, but she did admit that it made her feel a little better. We all knew exactly what she meant.

Possibly by reading this, it may serve to give you a fraction of what another parent with similar lives can provide for you. Please know that you absolutely are NOT alone! Even if you don't know anyone personally, trust me—we are here!

"Gee, he's good when he's with us." Joan told me once that my tombstone should have that written on it because I heard it so often.

Thank you, Joan, for seeing us as good parents in difficult and often unmanageable situations. You brought us together so that we could share our difficulties and we would know that we weren't alone. We all had children with symptoms that were severe—but amazingly, we weren't the only ones. Thank you, Joan, for providing us with opportunities to cry with people who could relate and laugh at the absolute absurdities of our lives which only we could really, truly understand and appreciate.

Additional thanks to Mary, Don, Sandy, Sharon, Gary, and Marilyn, our fellow "severe support group" members who allowed us to have momentary experiences of normalcy and the assurance that we weren't bad parents.

- 14 -

EFFECT ON OUR FAMILY

"Has this experience made your marriage stronger?" It always surprised me when someone asked me this and, believe it or not, it happened frequently.

It seemed like such a ridiculous question. I didn't have enough strength to take care of myself, when and how was I supposed to find the strength to give Tony support? I continue to be befuddled when people imply that a couple, whose child has a disability which results in extreme difficulties, would somehow end up with a stronger marriage. I just find this to be an odd notion. The answer to their question, for us, was always the same—absolutely not.

Tony and I coped in very different ways. My way included working for human service agencies, volunteering for the local newspaper and seeing my own therapist. Tony's way was to build outbuildings. We have 15 acres; approximately three-quarters of that is wooded. Part of his "therapy" was building a cabin back in the woods by hand, without the use of electric tools.

After the cabin came a shed for storing firewood, an extension to the shed to house our tractor, and another extension for tools. He built a garage and then an addition to that. He never suggested that I was spending too much of our money paying my therapist; I never suggested that he was spending too much time building additions onto sheds I wasn't convinced we really needed.

We recognized that it would be a good idea to pay attention to our marriage, but there is just so much energy available to survive day in and day out. We tried to take care of ourselves individually, but seldom did we have any additional strength to provide support for each other.

Our marriage did survive and I credit that to various things; although I doubt that it became stronger. The day after day, after week, after month, after year of exhausting and overwhelming stress was not conducive to building a better relationship. We were living with difficulties that were so extreme, even professionals couldn't provide us with answers. To make the assumptions that this helped our marriage seems, at least to me, unrealistic and a little bizarre.

Perhaps for some couples, this does make their marriage stronger. I can understand that a brief crisis of some sort may result in two people pulling together, making their relationship stronger. But when the difficulties and stress last for years with only rare and brief breaks, this does not seem to me to be a formula for a closer relationship. I'm sure that there are exceptions—and that is awesome—but it wasn't us.

We all hear, statistically, that a couple whose child has a chronic disability is more likely to get divorced. So why do some marriages stay intact while other marriages don't? I don't know.

One positive thing we did, is that neither Tony nor I focused on whose fault this was. We didn't wonder whose genes were responsible. It never seemed to be important and, most likely, the genes came from both of us. We now recognize we both have some tics, a little obsessive compulsiveness and can see similar traits in members of our extended families. But would it help Matthew, our other children, our marriage or our family if we knew whose genes were responsible? NO. It only leads to 'the blame game' that helps no one. Why devote any of our limited energy to a question that would serve no purpose and would, most likely, cause further stress and strain on our marriage? It just didn't seem to be productive.

This is not to say that we agreed on everything and didn't have arguments and difficult years. Heaven knows there were many times when total exhaustion and frustration resulted in taking it out on each other. There were times one or the other of us would get stuck in the notion that as parents, we needed to punish Matthew or participate in senseless arguments with him. We were only human; we got tired and acted in ways that were not useful for anyone. We sometimes disagreed on how one of us had responded to a specific incident. There were times when we barely spoke to each other and were more "partners" than a couple.

For so many years, we experienced other people throwing blame at us—we didn't need to do that to ourselves or each other. It was more like we circled the wagons. At times there were other wagons in our circle but most times it was just the two of us protecting our family and our children.

When punishment or rewards didn't work, we had no clue what else *to* do. Since I was going to conferences and learning, as well as the natural instincts that go along with mothering, I was able to more easily adapt my parenting methods and recognize that the philosophy of consequences, either positive or negative, wasn't working. I learned from reading and attending conferences about looking at symptoms differently and the benefits of proactive supports instead of reactive punishment.

Tony wasn't attending conferences or doing research. It was more difficult for him to let go of the old fashioned way of parenting. Since it is not our society's custom for the child to have the last word during a disagreement, there were numerous times that he and Matthew engaged in a yelling match, and both demanding the other to just stop talking. It reminded me of the classic power struggle in the movie, "Breakfast Club," in which the student and teacher are yelling at each other even though both want to stop. Much like our situation, both needed the last word. Like them, both Tony and Matthew wanted the exchange to end, they both wanted to stop—but neither could.

It was our job as parents to raise Matthew to be a good person who respected adults and authority figures. Neither of us was confident as to how to pull this off, though. And we never sat down at the end of a long day to discuss what we were doing wrong because we didn't know any alternatives. We became frustrated with ourselves and with each other. This, of course, impacted our marriage.

Another helpful factor was that we didn't have conflicts regarding medications, doctors, or educational approaches. In some ways it was more productive that Tony pretty much left those decisions up to me. Yet, while it helped not to have disagreements about these important decisions, it also put a great deal of stress and responsibility on me. I went to doctors' appointments and all of the school meetings. Tony felt that I was the one who had done the research, attended lectures and had educated myself about this disorder; therefore he left the decisions regarding treatment and school issues to me. To his credit, when I had made a poor choice, or when a decision blew up in our faces, he never blamed me or second guessed my decision. We just moved on.

Early in our marriage we had decided that when our first child was born, we were willing to make sacrifices so I could be a stay-at-home mother. By the time Matthew was born, I had not worked outside the house for seven years. I took care of the home and family while Tony earned the money, took care of cars, and brought our garbage to the dump. We never really discussed it. People who know me now may be surprised, but that's the way it was. As I said, our lives were pretty normal and uninteresting—even old fashioned—before Matthew.

On the other hand, we did tag team for each other at times. We often talked about the fact that one of us could never be a single parent. We recognized that keeping our marriage intact, while not always as solid as we would like, was important for everyone. We both recognized that we needed a partner in this vital and challenging job of raising all of our children under these extraordinary circumstances. There were years when our marriage, as is true for many families of children with chronic and significant difficulties, took a backseat to getting through a day, a week, a month and a year.

Tony and I felt that this was a period of time that we needed to survive—somehow. Survival was what we focused on. Survival for ourselves, our other children, for Matthew and for us. Just survive. Nothing fancy or special—simply survive. My therapist once told me that when someone is struggling to keep their nose above water, they don't do any fancy strokes. They do whatever needs to be done to survive. We were struggling to keep our own and our children's noses above water; fancy wasn't happening.

That doesn't mean, however, that there weren't times when both of us wondered if we would be able to continue. We are only human and sometimes it was just too much. It seems to me that we would have been extremely abnormal if the thought of packing a bag and leaving hadn't crossed our minds occasionally.

I remember one particularly difficult time when Matthew's OCD led him to regularly swear at Tony because he was "breathing wrong." This was extremely challenging and draining for Tony. He would come home from work, put his briefcase down and breathe. Matthew would swear at him and yell, "Why are you breathing that way? STOP! JUST STOP, YOU FUCKING PIG!" Someone suggested that I title this book, "Heaven Forbid My Husband Should Breathe."

Tony began to tell me that he just didn't know if he could do this any longer, and that he might need to leave. After having heard this one too many times on a day that had exhausted me, I said, "If you are going to leave, then leave. Stop talking about leaving and just leave." I turned and looked him square in the eyes and said, "BUT, if you leave me now, know that you will burn in hell for all eternity." He looked at me; we laughed...he stayed.

Social workers and therapists told us that we needed to take care of our relationship by having a date once in a while. We lived an hour from any city and 30 minutes from the closest restaurant. Occasionally we waited until Matthew was asleep and left our daughter in charge. This was pre-cell phone era, so we gave her the phone number of the restaurant being fairly confident that Matthew would not wake up after he had fallen asleep. He was typically exhausted by the end of the day, so once he was asleep he would generally not wake up until morning.

So again, what's the magic answer for how we stayed together? I don't know—we just did. The only explanation I can see as a possibility is that we loved our children more than anything. So whether Tony and I loved (or even liked) each other at any given time didn't really matter. Leaving my children was absolutely not an option. I'm sure it wasn't for Tony either. Additionally, I couldn't imagine being the only parent! It would be impossible, totally beyond my comprehension. If I accepted that I couldn't survive as the only parent, then I couldn't do something that would leave Tony in that same position. So we stayed together because we had to! For us there wasn't another option.

People ask me now if we think our experiences made our marriage stronger. I still answer the same way—I don't think so. Whenever Tony and I discuss those times (which is not very often) we always say the same thing—how did we do it? And again the answer is the same; we don't have a clue.

Things that helped: a few therapists who 'got it', availability of hospitalization, supportive doctors, and our commitment to being parents who were not willing to give up or stop believing in the positive attributes of our son. It's always been obvious that Matthew was and continues to be an amazing example of the resiliency of the human spirit. Knowing that helped us a great deal.

My biggest regret is that I didn't spend more one on one time with Jeff and Erika. Somehow they managed to not only survive, but to turn into the most decent adults I know. There were times when I was concerned how their childhood would impact their choices for spouses. Thankfully, they both chose the most wonderful people with whom to share their lives. And even more amazingly, both of them, Jeannie and Dan, sincerely enjoy being members of our family! It was an extremely difficult childhood for all my children but somehow they all grew up to be hard working, fun loving and decent adults.

I really don't know how all our children turned out so well. We had family therapy and I think that helped. Maybe the fact that they saw that Tony and I continued to support Matthew regardless of what was happening somehow conveyed to them that every member of this family would be loved unconditionally.

My son, Jeff, probably won't be thrilled that I say this because he is a sports kind of guy, but he has always been a caring and sensitive son. I remember many times when I was sitting on the front porch steps with my head in my hands, exhausted and frustrated at my inability to help Matthew. Pretty soon, Jeff sat next to me. He wouldn't say anything; he didn't need to. What could a 12 year old boy say in this situation?

Since his passion was sports, I attempted to play catch with him; I was much better with baseball than football. Bowling was an area in which I had at least some abilities so he and I spent many afternoons at the bowling alley—just the two of us. Because of Jeff's encouragement, the whole family spent many hours playing 'Pig' or 'Around the World' with the basketball hoop that was mounted to the back of our woodshed. Tony and Jeff often rode their bikes down or hiked through our woods to Hemlock Lake to go fishing.

One day when Jeff was six years old, he and I were on our way home from church. I asked him, "How come you decided to be born such a great kid?" Without missing a beat he said, "I figured you needed a break."

Jeff is now married to Jeannie, and is a History teacher, coach, father of Alessio and Sofia and I am happy to say, lives only 45 minutes away.

My daughter, Erika has always been artistic and creative. She spent many hours making projects. From an early age, she would write and illustrate these wonderfully amusing short stories. Since she was never much of a country girl, our big day out together always included Dan's Crafts and Things to buy materials for a new project. The two of us enjoyed putting jigsaw puzzles together, gluing them and hanging them up around the house.

Erika is married to Dan, lives too far away from us and invented a process of making incredibly beautiful pieces of art that you have to see to appreciate.

But to be specific and say what *precisely* worked for our family isn't something I can do. I think it is very complex and multi-layered. All I know is that each day we put one foot in front of the other and in the end, as individuals, we all survived and, as a whole, our family survived. Every single day I am incredibly grateful that we continue to have a loving family that truly enjoy each other's company.

JOANN McDERMOTT

Joann would become one of the most important counselors our family worked with; however, it almost ended before it began.

We started seeing JoAnn when Matthew left Crestwood. As part of the agreement when Matthew left residential and went into foster placement, we were required to see one of their off-site counselors. At the end of the third session, she said to us, "Mr. and Mrs. Giordano, I must tell you that your son's behaviors have nothing to do with his Tourette syndrome." She paused and then asked us, "Is my saying that going to impact my ability to work with you?" Neither of us said anything. I wanted to scream, "DAMN IT! You seemed different from the other social workers we had in the past." But instead, I said that I would think about it and let her know the next time we met.

The majority of people who had counseled us said the same thing in one way or another, just not quite so directly. But I had hoped that things would be different with JoAnn. She had told us that her husband was a bio-psychiatrist—or something like that. I didn't know specifically what he did, but I assumed it meant he knew something about brain chemistry and how it can impact behavior. After spending only three sessions with her, I had the impression that she was different from other social workers we had worked with. I thought that she was someone who we could educate about the complexities of Matthew's diagnoses and how easily symptoms could be misinterpreted as being purposeful misbehavior.

As I considered what she said and how I would answer her, I thought about the exact words she had used. She didn't use our first names or our son's name, which I thought was odd. Because she phrased it, "I must tell you," it occurred to me that there was a strong possibility that she had been instructed to tell us this and it didn't actually reflect her own thoughts.

The following week's session began with the same question—would her statement interfere with her ability to work with us? I told her that it would. I asked her how she could possibly help us if her explanation for our difficulties were based on the false assumptions that Matthew's behaviors had nothing to do with his diagnosis of Tourette syndrome. I had spent years blaming myself, assuming that I must be doing something wrong. I was past that and unwilling to jump back into the deep hole of self-blame that led nowhere and didn't help anyone.

I don't remember the rest of our conversation. All I know is that by the time we left, I was once again confident that she was open to learning what we were dealing with and helping us discern more productive ways to parent Matthew. I was willing to accept that we needed to learn *different* parenting strategies—but not *better* ones because that implied that what we were doing was bad!

We received support from JoAnn for over eight years. There was a time when JoAnn was seeing Matthew for individual therapy, the rest of us for family therapy as well as Tony and I for couples therapy. Not only was she instrumental in Matthew's success, she also was important for Erika and Jeff, and for Tony and me and our marriage.

She helped our marriage because she was able to be an objective observer. With her help, we were able to talk honestly about our feelings and to have conversations, which due to exhaustion and defensiveness, were impossible without her. I see this as being a critical component to us remaining not just married but together as a couple.

She saw us as a family with a problem and not as a bad family, or even as a family with a great kid whose parents needed fixing. I thank her for being open to learning about families like us—families that, I suspect, she didn't learn a great deal about in college.

Last year, Matt and I urgently needed her once again to help us discuss the painful topic related to his placements as a child. She knew our history, knew both of us as individuals and knew our family. Once again she was there for us and willing to be the person who helped us hear each other. Thank you, JoAnn for putting aside preconceived notions and opening your mind and your heart so that you saw us for who were; a good family in a difficult situation.

- 15 -

Teachers on Our Team

"Students don't *care* how much a teacher *knows* until
they *know* how much a teacher *cares*."
- Author unknown

We were terrified to go to Matthew's first open house. He
had not yet been diagnosed, but we were well aware of the
difficulties at home. We assumed that they were also part of his
school experience.

As we drove to the school, we wondered if his teacher would
even talk to us or would she avoid us? Would she hint at what
terrible parents we were, that we needed to punish him more; or
were punishing too much? We didn't know what to expect, but
we were fairly certain that it wasn't going to be remotely similar
to the open house experiences we were used to for our older
children. We sat outside her room waiting for our appointed time.
We entered the room with our heads down, feeling like we had
been sent to the principal's office.

Much to our surprise, his teacher, Mrs. Walker, greeted us
and told us what a wonderful, bright, friendly and cooperative
little boy Matthew was. We thought that possibly she had us
confused with some other student's parents. At the time, we
weren't aware that some youngsters are able to suppress
symptoms all day at school and then explode at home. We told
her our names and she assured us that she was speaking about our
son, Matthew Giordano. She told us that the only difficulties he
had in school were in understanding the concepts "before" versus

"after" and "over" versus "under." We could handle that! Ha! No big deal!

Our experiences with the majority of his teachers were positive. I recognize that this is not true for many parents who struggle to have educators understand these complex symptoms. Too often, educators make assumptions about symptoms that involve challenging behaviors and often punish rather than to provide support.

I continue to believe that the large majority of teachers truly want to do what's best for students. When their best intentions aren't enough for a specific student, all too often they are at a loss as to what else to try. That's why I saw it as important to educate Matthew's teachers in a positive fashion at any opportunity I had.

It's not unusual for parents to hear that the best way to get services for their child is to go to school meetings prepared for a fight. In my experience, if you go looking for a fight, too often you will find one, and that doesn't encourage a collaborative relationship to best serve the needs of the child. Considering the hard-to-understand nature and inconsistent variety of symptoms, it is no surprise that it works best when families and educators work together as a team. I didn't have *The Answer*, but I desperately wanted his teachers to have one. It didn't take long for me to recognize that teachers didn't have one either. Maybe as a team we could figure out something that would be helpful for Matthew.

Trust me, I know that developing a positive and collaborative relationship with schools is not always easy and occasionally even appears to be impossible. But, blaming someone isn't going to endear them to your child and, in the long run, my goal was to have teachers enjoy working with my child and delight in helping Matthew find success.

Since I wanted Matthew's teachers to be creative in providing supports, I wanted them to see him as a child and not a diagnosis. Providing them with a one page description with a nice picture attached can be a good strategy. By briefly listing strengths, difficulties and strategies that have and have not worked, the teacher enters the relationship with a child with basic but positive information. Making sure that this is included in the substitute teacher folder can prevent misunderstandings and avoided some devastating situations.

Additionally, no matter what was happening between me and the school, I tried very hard to not let Matthew see even a hint of any problems that may have existed. School was already a scary place for him. I, of course, wanted him to know that I had his back but also that the people at school were there to help us. They weren't enemies of mine or his. If he thought there was hostility, he would have been more anxious, which increased symptoms, and everything would have been more difficult. If I experienced any anger toward a teacher, he never knew it. Again, I recognize that this is not always easy, but it is important.

We were extremely fortunate that the majority of the school staff liked Matthew and provided positive supports. The fact that his symptoms were so obvious helped him because there was little doubt that he had Tourette syndrome. For the most part, there wasn't any question as to whether he was purposely being disruptive or that the behaviors might be attention seeking. So in a strange way, the level of his symptoms helped him in school— at least with the adults.

Matthew was very sensitive and intuitive as to how people responded to him. He frequently told me that a certain teacher didn't like him. I made attempts to let this teacher know in a manner that wasn't confrontational. I usually began the conversation by assuring them that I understood this was *his* perception and not necessarily what had occurred. But it was also important that they recognized that *his* perceptions were *his reality*. Fortunately things typically turned around fairly quickly because his teachers generally made an effort to reach out to him which renewed Matthew's desire to please the teacher.

Teachers matter! Think back on teachers who made a difference in your life. Almost all of us can remember at least one who impacted us in a positive fashion. Teachers do make a major difference.

This in no way is intended to encourage parents to immediately blame a teacher in subjects where the child is failing. Neurological disorders are extremely complex and difficult for everyone. Matthew did very well or poorly in classes depending on the level of his symptoms as well as his specific learning disorders. I met with his teacher attempting to determine the best approach, but I also never gave up on him—even when he had momentarily given up on himself.

I return to Ross Greene's philosophy in his extraordinarily valuable book, *The Explosive Child*. "It's our explanation of the behavior that leads directly to how we respond to it." It's very basic. If our explanation for a child's action is that he is deliberately being difficult and bad, we tend to punish. If, however, our explanation for a child's actions is that he *has* difficulties which are impacting him, we are much more likely to provide support. Having teachers see Matthew as a child *with* a difficulty became a major goal of mine.

ERIN LANE—FIRST GRADE

Miss Lane was incredibly accepting of Matthew's symptoms even though they increased and were changing dramatically week to week. Students however, began to tell him to be quiet. They stared at him, yelled at him to stop and began imitating his symptoms. With absolutely no knowledge or encouragement on my part, Matthew asked Miss Lane if he could tell the class about Tourette syndrome so they wouldn't tease him or yell at him so much.

Miss Lane sat in her rocking chair; she placed my little boy on her lap, put her arms around his waist and he told his classmates about Tourette syndrome. Loving, Nurturing, Supportive! That is precisely what all children need and for the most part, what my son received from so many people throughout his years in school.

Years later, I saw Miss Lane and I told her how critical that type of support was for him. She said what she had not told me was that Matthew shared with the class that sometimes, at home, the Tourette even made him say the "F" word. One little girl raised her hand and asked, "Miss Lane, what's the 'F' word?" Without missing a beat, Miss Lane answered, "Frog."

Thank you, Miss Lane.

STEFANIE PIRAINO—SECOND GRADE

Mrs. Piraino is everything a parent would ever want in a teacher!

Second grade was the year that symptoms went off the charts and things went to hell at home. The aggression increased; the episodes were more frequent and significantly more disruptive and dangerous. The tics and obsessive-compulsive behaviors were extreme and resulted in situations that were impossible to manage.

There were no good days; only very, very difficult ones for everyone—but mostly difficult for Matthew. There were times when anything could set him off when he was at home and sometimes even in public places with my husband or me.

Over the years, some people suggested I home-school Matthew. I believe that this is a positive option for many children. But, having him at school was the only time of peace for him and me. It also was the only time he had to be with other children, learning social skills and figuring out ways to manage his symptoms so he could remain in the general education setting and develop friendships.

In hindsight, I don't think it's a coincidence that symptoms became more prevalent as school work became more challenging. Even with all Mrs. Piraino's creative, nurturing support, she could not eliminate the additional academic demands that increased his stress and his symptoms, which in turn increased his stress, and on and on.

Mrs. Piraino never made me feel as if anything that I confided to her was my fault. She became an important member of our 'team'. She let me know what was occurring in school, which helped me and his doctors monitor trends and symptoms. Most importantly, I could talk to her without fear of being judged. This allowed me to be honest regarding how the day had begun prior to school, which helped her select the best approach when interacting with him that day.

Back then, I knew *nothing* about special education. I assumed that in a smaller classroom, he would be provided the support he needed and that he wouldn't have received them if he remained in the general education setting with 25 other students. I asked her if she thought the school would be recommending a more restrictive placement for Matthew. Would he be bussed to a different school that was for students who had behavior and emotional difficulties?

She looked at me as if I had two heads and asked me why I was considering that. I said we assumed that he was disruptive to the other students and the school would send him to a more restrictive setting at some point. She told me that the other children were easily adjusting to his noises, even to his singing Jingle Bells most of the day. They just ignored him and carried on with their work. She assured me that Matthew was smart, was progressing at the same rate as the other children, and that it was in his best interest to stay in his home school in the general education setting.

Okay—sounded good to me!

If she had agreed that we needed to place him in another setting, I believe that it would have put us on a fast track to disaster. Twenty years ago the large majority of these programs relied primarily on a strict consequence or reward-based philosophy. This would have made our situation so much worse. Matthew required a program that was positive and proactive and taught him strategies for managing symptoms instead of being reactive and punishing for symptoms. We also thought it was important for him to remain in a setting in which, if he wanted to have friends, he would need to learn strategies that would help him accomplish this.

Mrs. Piraino was instrumental in helping me determine at an early age the importance of walking that fine line regarding when we punish, when we teach, and when we ignore. It often remained a guessing game. Sometimes I guessed correctly; other times, not. But I recognized the importance of examining different approaches, knowing that stepping back and allowing my son to struggle was not always the wrong approach.

It was the end of the summer after second grade that Matthew was placed at RPC. Mrs. Piraino visited Matthew while he was there. We have told her numerous times how important that was to him and us. I will repeat it here. She was the only person, besides his family, who visited him while he was in placement. She brought him books as any good teacher would do, but she gave him much more. By visiting him, she communicated to him loud and clear that he was okay in her estimation and that she cared about him.

To this day, Matthew talks fondly of her and says that he would like to name his first daughter Stefanie in honor of his second grade teacher. I think that pretty much says it all!

JEAN GRIDLEY—SCHOOL PSYCHOLOGIST

In first grade, Matthew began to receive counseling services. After meeting with him for several weeks, Jean called and asked to meet with me. She showed me pictures that he had drawn during their meetings. They were incredibly intricate drawings of flowers. The detail was amazing.

She confided to me that Matthew was unlike any child she had worked with in the past. Remember, this was in the late 1980 when very few children were accurately diagnosed as having neuro-behavior disorders. She asked me for any resources that would provide her with some information about his diagnoses.

Jean conducted Matthew's first psycho-educational evaluation that year. The testing created a huge amount of stress for Matthew, and during the testing he began to display symptoms that shocked her. He hid under the desk and inside empty packing boxes, made noises and said words and phrases that were significantly inappropriate for the school setting. But she also saw a very bright, talented, personable and hard-working youngster.

After discussing the results of his testing, which indicated my son's strengths and weak areas, she asked if she could give me a hug. She had tears in her eyes. She had gotten to know him and understand the difficulty this little boy experienced. I was touched deeply that she was so moved by our situation.

In the years to follow, Jean continued to play a major role in Matthew's success at school and in the community. She even invited him to her home to play with her two sons and to join them at local festivals and parades. This made a lasting impression on him and he still cherishes those memories.

ROCHESTER PSYCHIATRIC CENTER SCHOOL

After three years of positive supports from caring teachers in his home school, Matthew spent the first half of third grade at the Rochester Psychiatric Center (RPC) children's unit. Due to ignorance regarding his diagnosis, he was punished for his vocal and physical symptoms. He lost points that were necessary to earn the reward of a home visit. He was told to sit in the corner when he did his tics. He suddenly hated school. How could this be happening to my son, who had always been a sponge for information and loved school?

I talked to the teacher, to other staff, but nothing changed. I was told that this was an important component of the total therapy package that was being provided to him. I saw it as a 'cookie cutter' approach that was rigid and didn't leave room for thinking outside the box to meet my son's individualized needs.

Clearly something had to change. He had been placed in the residential care for difficulties at home, not school. School had always been a positive environment. It only made sense that he be bused to his home school during the day and back to the children's unit for the evening until he was able to return to living at home. My role as an advocate needed to ratchet up, so I contacted Carol Godsave, the Chairperson for Special Education, at his home school.

CAROL GODSAVE, CHAIRPERSON FOR SPECIAL EDUCATION

I requested a meeting with the chairperson of special education at Matthew's home school and told her my plan for him to return. She scheduled a committee meeting and the team found no reason why that would be a problem. Carol told me that if a fan club with t-shirts could be allowed at a school, there would be one for Matthew. They welcomed him back with open arms. At the time, I was delighted to hear how popular he was with the teachers and staff.

After the meeting, one of the people at the meeting told me privately that children's residential units never allowed anything like this in the past, and she was confident that they wouldn't allow it for my son either. She explained that because Matthew attended their school, they received state funding. Her experience over the years had convinced her that they would not be willing to give that up.

If something makes such perfect sense, I'm typically not discouraged by people telling me that it can't happen. So I scheduled a meeting with Dr. Emami, the lead psychiatrist at the children's unit. I had known him for three months and experienced him as a gentle, kind, compassionate and intelligent person.

At first he told me that the school day was part of the treatment plan and Matthew could not miss out on that. I told him about my son being penalized for his symptoms. We talked about the fact that other than his symptoms, he was a good student and the behaviors they saw were due to inappropriate punishment. I also pointed out that my son could not receive the same level of education at their facility as he would in a general education setting. I was concerned that the longer he remained away from his home school, the more he would fall behind academically, making it even more difficult when he returned.

I shared with Dr. Emami that I had checked with the home school and they were more than happy to have him return. They had agreed with me that it would be good for him to stay in touch with his school friends and to receive an education that focused on academics instead of behavior management.

Dr. Emami eventually agreed, but said that the home district would need to pay for the cost of transportation, which was 40 miles one way. Since Carol Godsave and the rest of the team had seemed so eager to have Matthew return, I saw this as a tiny detail that just needed to be worked out. (It's sometimes helpful to be naïve!) I asked for another meeting with the special education team so that this plan could be put into place.

I walked into the meeting confident that my son would soon return to his school. The team agreed to change the paperwork to reflect that he was once again a student at his home school. Then the topic of transportation came up. I told them that Dr. Emami had said the school would provide transportation. Carol responded by saying that the school was not responsible for this because Matthew no longer lived within the school district's area.

It's difficult to put into writing how that simple statement touched off a fire storm deep within my parenting gut. My emotional 'baggage' flew open! I leaned into the table, not hiding my anger, stared directly into her eyes and said in a very emphatic manner, "My son LIVES at home—he is currently hospitalized in the city but LIVES at his home, which is most certainly within the school district's area."

Now I recognize that she had pushed a major button of mine and my emotions came out full force. In that instant, I didn't care about the law or all the positive supports that Carol had made possible up to that moment. The mama bear had emerged and my claws were out. I don't remember much about the meeting after that; however I walked away with a copy of the New York State Special Education Regulations, which clearly stated that they were not responsible for bussing. Bottom line, I didn't care who paid for it, I just wanted it to happen—NOW!

I showed the Special Education Regulations to Dr. Emami and the next thing I knew, Matthew was attending his home school. Some entity paid for his transportation. I didn't really care who; it was done and that was all that mattered.

I'm certain that it wasn't my angry reaction at the school meeting that made this occur. Instead, I am convinced that doing my homework ahead of time, being persistent, providing facts and meeting individually with people responsible for the decision were the important elements that led to the successful outcome. I was fortunate that Carol shared a desire to see Matthew succeed, as she demonstrated numerous times during the years that he was in school. She genuinely believed in his abilities.

She was the person who suggested that I check out the Norman Howard School, which provided the supports that he required even though it cost the school district additional funding. Carol was always dedicated to determining students' needs and doing what she could to provide for them.

The first week Matthew was at his home school, I was told that he would be the only youngster at the children's psychiatric unit to have homework because no one else was attending a school outside the hospital setting. They asked me how I wanted to handle this. I said, "He'll do his homework." He never complained about doing it either. Amazingly, even at such a young age, he knew that being the only kid that had homework was worth it if that was what it took to be in his own school.

A few of the dedicated people at the children's unit helped him every evening with his homework. If it didn't get done, his teachers understood and didn't punish or reduce his grade because of it. The plan was working!

LINDA ERHARDT—FOURTH GRADE

I have to admit that I was concerned when Matthew was assigned to her class. We all live in the same very small community and I knew her to be a rather proper woman. How was she going to handle his tics, particularly his new one?

The summer before fourth grade, he developed a vocal tic that remains, to this day, to be the *worst* he has had in his 29 years of life. It was "Fuck you, God." How on earth would this very nice woman tolerate this type of symptom? I got a few more grey hairs just thinking about it!

I met with Mrs. Erhardt a few days prior to the beginning of school to discuss Matthew's strengths, Tourette syndrome and to give her examples of some of his current symptoms. But, I just couldn't sit there and tell her the phrase that was his current vocal tic. It's not a word that I was comfortable saying, even after hearing it numerous times every day all summer. I was hoping beyond hope that it would change prior to school beginning, or that somehow he would be able to suppress this tic until after school. I just couldn't say it to her. I figured she would hear it soon enough.

So off he went to school; I had my fingers and all of my toes crossed. I waited for the phone to ring. I knew that Mrs. Erhardt was most likely hearing him say it daily. It was his primary vocal tic at the time and suppressing it all day just wasn't feasible, no matter how much I wanted that to be possible.

No phone call. No note from school. No calls from RPC saying that the teacher had said something to them about inappropriate language. Nothing!! And I wasn't picking up the phone to ask if she had heard anything new lately.

It wasn't until mid-October that I finally learned the truth about what was happening in school. I was at the local mall doing some shopping and ran into Mrs. Erhardt. She told me something had occurred that day which she never would have believed would happen as long as she was a teacher.

She was giving a lesson on Alexander Graham Bell. She asked the class, "What did Alexander Graham Bell say after inventing the phone?" The class was very quiet; no one seemed to know the answer. She encouraged someone to take a guess.

Matthew's vocal tic came out loud and clear, "Fuck you, God." She responded by saying "No, not that. Does anyone have any other suggestions?"

We all know that she could have had a very different reaction! She could have told him to go to the principal's office. He could have been in serious trouble. But she didn't punish him. What she did was to communicate to him, no questions asked, that he was okay. And just as importantly, she modeled for the other students that he was okay. They knew they weren't allowed to say those words, but she taught them something even more important. Matthew was different and different is fine. They didn't have Tourette syndrome and he did—no big deal.

I'm certain that she must have heard that phrase said softly or maybe under his breath enough times that her explanation by that time was that this was a symptom and it was just words. Nothing more.

She demonstrated that fair is not necessarily equal and equal is not always fair. The most unfair treatment is to treat everyone equally. Giving everyone what they need—now *that* is fair. Consider a child who has a cold. If we were to treat everyone equally, we would either give *everyone* a tissue or no one would be allowed to have one, not even the student who needs it. Unfortunately when it comes to behaviors (or symptoms that appear to be behaviors) it is much more difficult to recognize what is fair and what is unfair.

The wonderful thing about this story is that no one made a big deal over it. Her answer was immediate and calm, demonstrating that it really was no big deal.

Thank you, thank you, thank you, Mrs. Erhardt. Your *explanation* was that Matthew was a good young boy who had a disorder and, therefore, what he said was not cursing or inappropriate; it was just a symptom—nothing more!

KAREN (LABRUTTO) LAHR—CRESTWOOD CHILDREN'S CENTER

Thinking 'outside the box' can be critically important when supporting youngsters. Thinking *way* outside the box is second nature to Karen.

The summer he was living at Crestwood Children's Center, Matthew attended their school program. We weren't sure what to expect even though our experience with the majority of the other staff at this facility had been very positive.

At the time, one of his symptoms was to slam a chair on the floor repeatedly while saying, "God damn-it, you mother fucker" precisely at the same time the chair hit the floor. He said that he needed to do this until the chair hit the floor with a certain pitch. This school only had plastic chairs. Not surprisingly, Karen was afraid that a piece of plastic could easily break off and hurt another student. She asked Matthew if he thought duct taping a block of wood to his desk so that he could hit *that* with a wooden mallet instead of smashing the plastic chairs on the floor would work for him. He agreed to give it a try. It worked!

Karen told me that other staff members expressed their shock when they would walk by, hear the banging and see the other students continue to work as if nothing were happening. It doesn't surprise me because kids can be very adaptable. It's often us adults that have a difficult time adjusting our way of thinking, or believing that kids will be able to accept something that we find so unusual.

When I called her recently to ask for permission to be included in this book, she confessed that prior to school beginning when she first saw the paper work for Matthew, there was *NO* way she wanted this boy in her class. She didn't know anything about Tourette syndrome and didn't think she would be able to help him. She told me that after she met him, she realized that he was a cute little boy who had difficulties; nothing more.

Because of her total acceptance, it was just another day for her to come up with a strategy that supported Matthew while keeping everyone else safe. She is one of those incredible teachers who models acceptance so her students followed her example. No one ever teased or bullied him for behaviors that very easily could have been seen as being pretty weird.

Thank You, Karen!!

OTHER WONDERFUL TEACHERS

With only two weeks remaining in the school year, the eighth grade English and social studies teachers tutored Matthew after school. It had been a rough year and they knew that he would not pass the final exam without this extra tutoring. Because of them, Matthew *did* pass. Additionally, they both advocated for him at a critically important special education meeting when I didn't know what more could be done. I know that teachers often are reprimanded for this and I so appreciated what they did for me and, more importantly, for Matthew.

Linda Lawrence, Vice Principal, was more than willing to have Matthew nap in her office at the Norman Howard School when he became overwhelmed and exhausted. She always treated him with kindness and respect as well as helped other teachers understand his symptoms, his needs and his abilities.

Not all of his teachers were as nurturing or supportive.

There was a teacher who was committed to "breaking him" of what she interpreted as inconsistent "effort" with handwriting. It didn't matter that I told her the majority of youngsters with Tourette and ADD typically have significant difficulty with written language. This particular teacher was steadfast in her belief that his inconsistent handwriting was due to purposeful oppositional defiant behavior. She was determined that if Matthew could write legibly one time, he was capable of writing well every time. It just wasn't true, but she wouldn't believe me or the literature I provided, which reinforced the fact that she was mistaken.

I remember the day this teacher assigned homework that consisted of writing ten spelling words five times each. As Matthew attempted this assignment, it quickly became obvious that the only way this could be completed on this particular evening was if I wrote for him as he spelled the words verbally five times each. Even with this accommodation, it took over two hours to complete. Every few minutes he would screech, jerk his head backwards a specific number of times and hit his elbow against the wall. He also needed to jump up and down in a precise manner if these interfering symptoms occurred in the *middle* of attempting to spell one of the words.

The next day he returned from school with the words "Mom's Handwriting" and a grade of "0" written across the top of the paper...in red ink, of course. She continued to insist that if we were consistent in requiring him to write for himself, he would stop this bad behavior. She suggested, as many others had, that what he needed was a quiet spot and to ensure that he did his homework the same time of day, every day. Simple and logical solutions—that did not work.

Another support person told Matthew that he wasn't going to be able to go onto Jr. High school with his friends if he didn't improve his handwriting. She also warned him that he needed to stop doing weird things because he eventually wouldn't have any friends left.

I'm confident that both people meant these to be motivating. They weren't. They only increased his anxiety, and therefore, his symptoms and certainly didn't do much for his self-esteem.

No matter how good Matthew's education plan was, teachers made a huge difference. They ran the show. His success depended on their attitude, overall demeanor and even personality. They either fully demonstrated acceptance, or the message to him and other students was rejection. I am grateful to the majority of his teachers for their acceptance of my son.

MRS. STEWART

I can't end this chapter without mentioning a very special sixth grade chorus teacher. She offered to direct a musical that included every student from the entire sixth grade who was interested in being involved, including my son.

No one, not even Matthew, could guarantee that at any given moment during the performance he wouldn't yell out the same phrase that he had said when asked what Alexander Graham Bell had said after inventing the phone.

Despite that, this incredible teacher asked Matthew to play one of the lead roles. That meant that he would be on stage a good majority of the show and had lines to speak. Amazing! I will forever be grateful and impressed at the courage of this wonderful woman. That's what I call being supportive! In case you're wondering…not one single 'f' word was uttered by anyone on stage that evening!

Since this entire chapter talks about people, I will end it by paraphrasing a story that one of my co-workers, Kathy McCarthy-Proulx, relates during her presentations to educators and parents. She calls it the "Pearl Necklace" story.

Children have many doctors, therapists, teachers, counselors, bus drivers, school psychologists, cafeteria personnel, principals and other support people in their lives. There are numerous professionals who dedicate their lives to supporting children with disabilities and they can have a significant impact.

Kathy compares these professionals to the numerous pearls that are on a necklace. Each pearl represents the professional while the string represents the child. The string passes through each of the pearls. Because of that, the pearl influences the string and the string affects the pearl. Pearls are beautiful and very precious. We value and appreciate them.

However, it is the parent, represented by the clasp on the necklace, that holds it all together. Removing one of the pearls would change the necklace, but there are many more pearls to take its place. The string advances from one pearl to the next. They impact each other and both are important, but the string moves on to another pearl. Without the clasp, the necklace would fall apart. The all-important clasp is the parent who has been with the child from the beginning and will be there in the future.

Kathy relates a story of a young man who lived for sports in school—it was the main reason he remained in school. The end of the school year was approaching and he was failing math. The teacher asked to meet with his parents to discuss this and recommended that they remove the boy from all sports activities until he pulled his grades up.

The boy's mother considered doing this. But then she thought about who her son was. He had always struggled in math and certainly was not going to choose a profession that required a strong math aptitude. The mother thought about the success he experienced in sports and the satisfaction these successes provided him. She recognized the only thing that kept him engaged in academics was because he could also be involved in sports.

The mother knew that the teacher meant well, but she also knew her son much better than this teacher did. The mother decided to ignore the teacher's suggestions and instead have her husband spend extra time helping their son with math. The boy graduated and recently received a high honor in his career choice—one that doesn't involve math.

We parents certainly don't always know what is best, and often make mistakes; just ask my children. But we can't ignore our gut feelings, or parent intuition, whatever you want to call it. We, after all, have known our child longer than anyone else in the world and our voice should be heard and respected.

We also need to recognize that teachers spend many hours of the week and most of a year with our children. They see them, experience them and influence them in ways that we parents don't. I clearly recognized their importance in Matthew's life and, therefore, did whatever I could to educate them in a positive and effective manner. This included letting them know that I understood the demands that are placed on them and how difficult it is to teach a youngster with my son's challenges. I wanted them to know that I respected their input and their expertise. I tried to convey in every way I could that I considered us to be a team. We needed to work together at learning about these highly complex and misunderstood disorders to recognize the most effective approaches. It sometimes required me to swallow my emotional reactions and to be as patient as I could while they learned about my son and his needs. Even though at the end of the day, I was his parent and needed to make the decisions regarding his education, I also needed to recognize that the teachers also had expertise. Additionally, a major component to my son's success was that they liked him, and it was helpful if they also liked me.

Because of the encouragement and approval that many teachers gave him, Matthew grew up knowing that people believed in him, accepted him and, for the most part, didn't punish him for his symptoms. I am extremely grateful to those who were such important members of our team and recognize that your acceptance and support played a major role in Matt's success as an adult. Thank you.

- 16 -

MANAGING SYMPTOMS
AND LEARNING LIFE STRATEGIES

I want to relate a story, which I heard years ago, that helped me parent all my children.

"Why the Butterfly Died" is a story attributed to Henry Miller. In the story, a young boy in India walks up to a wise man that is holding a cocoon. The boy asks what it is and he's told that it is a cocoon with a butterfly inside of it. The man explains that the cocoon will soon split open so that the butterfly can emerge and fly away. The boy asks if he can have it. The wise man gives it to the young boy, but first makes him promise that under no circumstances must he do anything to help the butterfly come out of the cocoon.

The boy promises and takes the cocoon with him to a quiet place. He watches as a very small hole develops. He sees the butterfly fighting to break through. He watches as the butterfly struggles and pushes to break free of the cocoon. It appears to the boy that the butterfly is exhausted and might die if he does nothing to help. So the boy breaks away a small piece of the cocoon and with that little bit of help, the butterfly emerges.

The butterfly spreads its wings to fly but instead falls to the ground. The boy watches as the butterfly struggles to fly but finally it dies. Crying, the boy finds the wise man and confides in him what he has done.

The wise man is stern with the boy and tells him that for the butterfly to be able to fly, the wings need to be strengthened by beating against the cocoon while it struggles and fights its way out. Without this opportunity for the wings to become strong, the butterfly was not able to fly, fell to the ground and died.

This story helped me when I wanted to jump in and make Matthew's life easier. It reminded me that he was the one who needed to negotiate difficult situations so he would become strong. It's not easy as a mother to sit back and do nothing. But if I didn't let Matthew negotiate tough times by himself, I was denying him opportunities to learn ways to survive in a world that wouldn't necessarily provide him accommodations; a world in which he would need to know how best to approach many difficult situations on a daily basis.

On the other hand, over the years I also learned the importance of thinking about what can be done *for* the child prior to the episode instead of what will be done *to* him after. It's similar to the nursery rhyme, Humpty Dumpty. We know that once Humpty falls off the wall, all the king's horses and all the king's men won't be able to put him back together again.

I found that I needed to examine situations which repeatedly resulted in rage episodes and then to have discussions with Matthew, when things were calm. We discussed what we could both do so he didn't fall off the wall; or how we could help him down from the wall so he didn't break; or why he needed to get up on the wall in the first place. Was there something we both could do instead?

It still amazes and saddens me when I think about how many years went by before I first asked Matthew if there were something that we could do differently and then to strategize a plan of action. I was too caught up in me being the parent and he the child. Now, it makes so much sense to me that if we want a child to buy into using strategies, it's imperative that he or she be involved in developing them.

Penny, a wonderful mother I have gotten to know, recently told me that she was at a school performance when her child began getting extremely agitated and disruptive. She took him outside where she asked him if he could think of anything that might help him. He said that it sometimes helps him to walk around. They walked and he was able to calm down. This not only helped prevent that particular rage episode, it taught her son that using strategies can actually be useful. This may help him become open to developing and using more strategies in the future.

A few years ago I came across an excellent article that discussed the benefits of planning for the future instead of constantly processing the past. If I made any attempts at processing anything that had just occurred with Matthew immediately after the rage episode, he often returned to being smack in the middle of another meltdown. It took me way too long to realize the benefits of waiting and later discussing strategies for the future with him instead of focusing on the past. He didn't want to lose control. What could I do to help? What could he do instead? Was there anything that might help reduce his level of anxiety? What could we do that would help him to learn different ways to manage symptoms that resulted in rage?

When Matthew was 12, he asked me if we could talk about something important. He told me that he hated when he said mean things to me or swore at me and he wondered if we could talk about ideas that might help him with this. I asked him to consider what would happen if he swore at other people. He said that the people wouldn't want to be with him. We agreed that since swearing was a symptom of Tourette, he should be able to do it at home as long it wasn't damaging others. He said it would be helpful if he could say anything he needed to say in the privacy of his room and I agreed. If, however, he swore directly at me, the plan was that I would walk away. I wouldn't say anything, just walk away. We had already discovered the benefit of my not continuing a difficult discussion as he became increasingly out of balance because it often resulted in a more heated debate with increased levels of negative emotions. From now on, I would just walk away. He thought this plan was a good idea as he was eager to learn ways to not swear at me because it resulted in emotional pain for him.

That evening when I was helping him with his homework, he called me a bitch. I closed the book and walked away. He apologized profusely; I kept walking. He apologized louder—I walked. He followed me yelling and swearing—I went into my bedroom, locked the door and blasted my radio so he would *think* that I couldn't hear him. He continued to kick the door, yelling at me. Because I walked away and didn't engage in the episode in any way, it ended much sooner.

It took a while, but he was highly motivated to manage this symptom. I don't know how he did it but he eventually did. It also reduced my constant state of anxiety by admitting that I couldn't control everything. I took care of me—he learned a strategy.

But wait a minute—haven't I said that punishing Matthew didn't work? Yes. Wasn't walking away from him a form of punishment? Somewhere along the way I figured out that there was a major difference between punishments that make no sense and natural consequences that taught him something. By walking away when he swore at me, Matthew recognized that swearing at someone resulted in that person not wanting to be with him. Therefore, my walking away made sense to him. That doesn't mean he liked it, or thought it was a swell idea in the moment— but it was a natural consequence instead of random punishment. I was disciplining him; not punishing. I recently looked up the Latin root for the words discipline and punishment. Punishment means to inflict pain while discipline means to teach. I am very in favor of discipline!

It's possible that our children will always have symptoms, but as their parents, we want them to have as typical lives as possible. This requires that they learn to manage symptoms, not avoid life activities when situations are difficult. It doesn't mean hiding from society every time symptoms are increased. This fine line is unique for every person. It is not easy for a parent or child to determine how to negotiate that line in a way that will always result in positive growth. We just do the best we can do at the moment.

Kathie Snow says, "If people are going to *Live* in the *Real World*, they must first *Learn* in the *Real World*." This statement often provided me with guidance as Matthew progressed into adulthood. I heard Kathie Snow discuss this concept in 1995 when I was attending the Partners in Policy Making training. Too often, we parents are so invested in protecting our children that we may not allow situations to evolve which can provide opportunities for them to learn how to live in the real world. Kathie Snow's website has many interesting insights and I would recommend checking it out.

Initially, I did what I could to prevent my son from experiencing more difficulties than he already had. Eventually, I came to realize that it was important for Matthew to have real life struggles, including situations that involved his symptoms, so that he could stumble, fall and pick himself up. This is how all kids learn. I knew that he needed to learn his own strategies to cope and manage his life and symptoms.

Matthew had to learn to live in the real world in ways so that his symptoms would interfere as little as possible. I needed to allow him those opportunities to learn how to do this. It was an extremely fine line between advocating for others to ignore his symptoms and allowing the experience of difficult and often painful situations which would help him learn to manage them so he would be prepared for a world that wouldn't be as tolerant or accepting.

By *managing symptoms*, I'm not suggesting that he needed to *stop or control* symptoms. There is a difference between stopping, controlling, and managing. The first two suggest that a person has power over the symptoms; the latter is using strategies that assist the person in finding ways to reduce the negative impact on his or her life.

I believed that if he stumbled and no one was there to pick him up, this would be the motivation he needed to discover *how* to pick *himself* up; it might teach him how to avoid stumbling quite so severely the next time. Most kids learn this without much effort. But for Matthew, this was much more difficult and required a gargantuan effort on his part. I was always amazed at his ability to maintain that effort even during extremely difficult years.

Managing symptoms also doesn't mean that I stop supporting my son. I so wish that there was a book with guidelines that tell us specifically when to protect, when to support and when to allow opportunities for growth. When do you; when don't you; how much; how little? When do I punish? When do I ignore? When do I recognize that he is just being a typical kid? When do I provide support? When do I teach? When do I let him learn on his own. At one time, I considered titling this book "The Fine Line." So *many* decisions are about walking a fine line; making an already difficult situation even harder!

SANDRA HOLLIS

I met Sandra after presenting at a conference, and she literally cornered me and asked if we could talk because she thought our sons were long distance twins.

I thank God for Sandra being at that presentation. As we talked, it became obvious that she was the mother of an incredibly intelligent, kind, charming, funny young man who had a very similar level of challenging behaviors as my son. We talked well into the night. It was amazing for both of us that we had found the mother of our son's "twin." This was, and continues to be, such a blessing for me.

Sandra and her husband decided when their son was very young, they would focus on using opportunities for learning how to *manage* his symptoms instead of using them as an excuse.

She told me that when Zak was very young he had a 'poking' tic. He had to poke things numerous times until it was 'done.' One day he was poking a little girl in his Sunday school class. The father of the little girl told Sandra what had occurred in a less than cheerful way. She told Zak that poking items was okay, but made it very clear that in no way was it *ever* okay to poke other people. She walked with him back into the classroom and made him apologize. It didn't matter if it was a result of his difficulty inhibiting his behaviors, it was inappropriate. Sandra wanted him to learn that this was not acceptable behavior and somehow he needed to figure out a way to manage his life so incidents like this would not reoccur. He did.

Our friendship has grown over the years because our sons are so similar. At one conference held in the D.C. area, our boys asked if they could go visit the museums while we were busy at the conference. Matt was 17 and Zak was younger, but since they were both good, responsible kids *and* they were going to an area with a great deal of supervision from police, we agreed. Our only worry was that they would get lost and not know how to get back to the hotel. We gave them plenty of extra money for food and to take a taxi both ways. We wrote down the name and address of the hotel on numerous pieces of paper and put them in many of their pockets. We also gave them one of our cell phones.

When they didn't return at the time we had told them to be back, we got a little worried. Pretty soon we saw them enter the lobby laughing. I asked Matt for the money that was left over since we had given them so much more than was needed.

They looked at each other smiling. Zak told us that they had used up most of the money on food during the day so had to take the subway instead of a taxi back to the hotel. They had asked someone at the station precisely how to do this; however they misjudged and got off at the stop for the Pentagon Building. At the time, Zak had a 'tic' that whenever he saw a rifle, he would need to touch the tip of it—definitely not a good symptom when in the vicinity of the Pentagon! They walked the last couple miles back to the hotel, very pleased with their adventures. Sandra and I still wonder *what* on *earth* we were thinking letting these two loose in Washington, D.C.

Our friendship transcends our sons' similarities but since Zak is so akin to Matt, it is such a blessing having Sandra in my life. She *really* understands and she loves my son exactly the way he is.

We live almost 2,000 miles apart, but we are 'sisters'. I can talk with Sandra about the wonderful times as well as those that are more difficult. Sandra knows! Our conversations include both tears and a bizarre type of humor. Sandra once suggested that we could be the co-presidents of the "Fuck you, Mom" club. Having a sense of humor is important—having a friend with a similar life and sense of humor is priceless.

If you find a relationship like this—hang on to it and count your blessings. I know I do!

- 17 -

WHEN IT'S OVER, IT'S DONE—*FOR THEM*

Matthew's symptoms involved an obsessive compulsive aversion to people breathing their germs near him, or sometimes even in the same room. Unfortunately this became particularly true of Tony's breathing. Matthew would often enter a room and if Tony were there, he needed to run from window to window breathing in the *clean air* until he was able to get to the next room. Eating dinner together became a huge challenge.

By this time Matthew, and I had discovered the benefits of thinking outside the box and developing strategies that were proactive. I asked him every night whether he was in a place where he thought he could eat at the table with all of us. If he felt like he needed to eat in another room, this was totally appropriate.

One particular evening, Matt miscalculated and believed that he could eat with us. He was *very* wrong and a huge meltdown ensued. He left the table and returned in 10 minutes. While the rest of the family was still reeling from the explosion, Matt came back to the kitchen happy and wanting to have a conversation about an upcoming holiday. Needless to say, no one was ready to talk about anything, particularly something pleasant.

How is it possible that so soon after an outburst is done, he acts as if *nothing* has happened? Matthew's neurological rages fluctuated in the length of duration, but one thing was almost always a given; when it ended, he was sincerely remorseful, apologize and then continue on as if nothing had occurred.

We most often had no idea as to the reason for the meltdown except that for whatever reason, a *need* of his wasn't being satisfied. By this time, we knew that it was never his *true intention* to hurt anyone and clearly it was related to his diagnosis. But, that didn't always help me or anyone who had been present during the meltdown get past it as quickly as he did.

It helped me to explain this phenomenon in the following way:

A child is *Calm* with *Balanced* neuro-chemistry. Something disrupts the brain chemistry and suddenly there is a strong *Need* that must be completed. The *Need* may result from an obsessive-compulsive symptom; a sensory issue; a complex tic; an impulsive action, or any number of unknowns. Until this *Need* is completed, the brain continues to be *out-of-Balance*, resulting in *Heightened Anxiety* which leads to rage or a meltdown. The child is finally able to complete the *Need* resulting in reduced *Anxiety*. Rage and meltdown behaviors disappear. The child is relieved and happy that his brain has returned to being *Balanced* and can once again be *Calm*.

But, it's a different story when other people, understandably, become agitated by the child's rage and or meltdown. Their brain chemistry also starts out as being *Balanced* until the child begins to have "behaviors" for, what they perceive to be, no apparent reason. Their brain goes from *Balanced* to *Mad*.

The child finally completes the *Need* and returns to being *Calm*. The other people are baffled as to how things could be so violent and horrible one minute, and then so quickly the child acts as if all the screaming, hitting, throwing of objects, etc. never occurred. Since their brains are now functioning in a *Mad* mode, they yell at the child, even though he is now back to *Calm* and *Balanced*.

The child wonders, "What's the matter with them? Why are they mad? It's not like I wanted to act this way. Everything is back to being okay now. It's over!" So when these other people remain *Mad* and yell at the child, punish or lecture him, the odds of the child staying *Balanced* are very slim. Instead, because people are yelling at and blaming him, the child's brain chemistry returns to *Unbalanced* and the cycle continues. It's absolutely understandable why other people respond in an angry manner, but…it doesn't work!

As I have said, Matthew always apologized, but it's not easy to accept a child's apologies immediately after a rage episode or meltdown. But, I was afraid that if Matthew thought that his apologies wouldn't be accepted, at some point he would stop apologizing. That would not only have been regrettable, it was frightening.

What helped me was to consider rage episodes as being similar to prolonged and loud burping, sneezing, vomiting and other things I find distasteful, but over which neither I nor Matthew had control. The only positive response on my part that had any chance of helping the situation was for me to remain calm. If I showed how angry I was, it resulted in Matthew being more anxious and significantly increased the odds that another meltdown would occur.

I knew Matthew hated saying and doing things that hurt people he loved. He often wanted reassurance of our continued love after these meltdowns. I admit that sometimes, I required my own *time-out* to regroup. It was hard to consistently remember that his actions were symptoms, and it was extremely difficult not to take them personally. Sometimes I was successful. Other times I wasn't. Things were better for everyone when I was.

It became easier when I developed a strategy to concentrate on remembering the extremes of his emotional responses. I tried to keep in mind that his emotional-swings were capable of fluctuation to very high intensity in both directions; his extraordinarily loving and kind nature as well as the severe neurological rage.

BETH RYAN

Beth has been my close friend since 1968 when we met at college. Over the years, she has remained my friend despite the fact that I didn't always make it easy for her. There were many times when I was too tired to call, write or visit her. When I did call, she listened without judgments or suggestions. By not offering 'support', she supported me in the best way possible. Thanks Beth, I love you!

- 18 -

TONY'S THOUGHTS

When I thought about writing a chapter for this book, I didn't know where to begin. It's such an overwhelming task. Do I start with the really difficult times, the good; the effect on Matthew, our other children, Kathy and me, friends, extended family? It obviously impacts the child with a diagnosis the most but I had to consider how it impacted other members of the family…each so differently.

After learning Matthew had this thing called Tourette syndrome, Kathy and I attempted to learn all we could about it—her more than me. Coming from an engineer's viewpoint, I knew how important it was to understand the many complicated aspects of this disorder, as well as the ramifications of all the related difficulties. This included not only my son's experiences living with these issues on a daily basis, but also how was I going to guarantee the safe family environment that a father is supposed to provide? This proved to be much harder than I ever thought was possible.

Aside from trying to obtain information, help, proper medication and all the other things that were necessary for a child and family who live with these conditions, there were other important aspects that entered into the picture, which I never would have given a thought to prior to this experience. One of those was the perception and understanding—or as it turned out, the misunderstanding—of everyone outside of our immediate family regarding what was happening to Matthew and to all of us. There has been a lot written about disorders similar to Tourette syndrome in the last 10 years, but there was very little available 25 years ago. It seemed as if everything we experienced was like plowing new ground, facing the unknown, learning about another symptom and another diagnosis that we needed to understand. And it had to be understood yesterday because we needed the information and skills immediately. There was no time for a learning curve.

Other people's understanding and knowledge about realities of these difficult symptoms was lacking and non-existent. It usually resulted in judgmental statements or sometimes just looking the other way and ignoring what we were experiencing.

Initially, when we were out in public, other people's reaction to Matthew's symptoms was difficult for me to experience. I had to work very hard at getting past other people's judgmental looks. I finally came to a place where it stopped being a big deal for *me* what other people thought, but I think it still was difficult for Matthew.

Because of our experiences, one thing I have definitely learned is to not judge another parent by their children's actions. For example, there frequently are times that while shopping in stores, we see a child who appears to be behaving badly. A common response is to judge the parent as not being in control of their child. I've learned that anyone witnessing this doesn't know the reality of the entire situation and, therefore, simply cannot presume to know what that parent needs to do to get their child under control. I've learned to never judge a parent by their child's behavior. I know all too well how that feels. It is demeaning, humiliating and just plain stinks!

Something that I needed to work hard on was when Matthew was losing control. Instead of stepping in as the disciplinarian, I needed to try to put myself in his place. I had to take many, many breaths in my attempts to recognize that he was doing the best that he could do at the moment. This was really difficult and took me several years. I tried to remind myself that we can't always control a sneeze like Matthew couldn't control his behaviors and you just have to deal with it.

There were many difficult situations we lived through in the best way we knew how. There were many bad days, but there were also many good times along with the struggles. I believe that each of us, and more so Matthew, are stronger individuals from the experiences of having to live and deal as a family with the challenges that these symptoms caused. I think every member of my family is stronger because we all needed to learn, cope, handle, laugh, cry, pray and on and on…with all the many different and often difficult situations. This is what makes a person who they are. I want to use a phrase like "well rounded," but, that implies a circle and there are just too many rough edges for that term to be appropriate. However, I think it may have provided us with tools and strategies that can be used as we face different types of future difficulties and struggles.

I was brought up by what I thought, at times, were fairly strict parents. But now as I've grown older, I have realized that they were not really strict, but instead were loving, caring and pretty smart parents. I guess we don't realize these things until we're a parent ourselves. We all learn from our parents, teachers, friends, people who weren't friends, life experiences, books, etc. Your life is what makes you who you are. There is no manual. There are too many variables. We all just do the best we can, try to learn and to do better next time.

When I was first a parent, I tried to rely on this vast pool of knowledge that I had acquired in my life up to that point. I was actually shocked and disappointed in myself that I didn't have all the information or knowledge that I needed to be 100 percent successful at parenting. I've tried to think things through, to analyze logically what needed to be done. When that didn't pan out the way I had intended, I needed to find other ways to parent.

It was always extremely difficult for me to have one of my children swear at me, call me names, and all the other things that happened because of Matthew's symptoms. My life had not prepared me for dealing with that. Probably the most upsetting times were when he would yell, scream and swear at Kathy or at me. This was the button that set me off the most. I have learned that this was the disorder and not my son being disrespectful to us; but it took me a very long time and it wasn't easy. I always had a hard time with this, not surprisingly. It took many years of telling myself over and over—"this is the disorder and not my son" until I finally had a better understanding—or maybe just more patience with it. It wasn't easy to remember that this was due to the disorder, particularly when it was happening.

One way I found that helped me deal with the difficulties that were part of our lives was to find a place where I could get away from it all. We have a bit of land with woods directly behind our house. One summer, I found myself actually considering the possibility of jumping into my car and driving west—1, 10, 100, 1000 miles. Just go and drive! I had to come up with a better option, so I decided to build a cabin back in our woods. During the course of one summer, I hand-carried 2 x 4's, 2 x 6's, 4 x 8 lumber, plywood sheets, shingles, windows and nails back to the cabin site in the middle of the woods. I was sometimes able to use a cart, but almost always materials were hand carried because the ground was wet and muddy. Additionally, there was no electricity out there so all sawing and drilling was by hand. This was 25 years ago and I didn't have battery powered tools back then. I built a 12 foot by 12 foot cabin with a Dutch door, three windows and a 4 x 12 foot porch. It included a wood stove, fold-up table and shelving.

The point is that I had to find something that would help my frame of mind. This provided me with physical labor but also gave me time to think and try to understand my life and my family. Later on, I used the cabin for overnight camp outs with my kids. It actually ended up providing a number of good memories as well as a place of regaining and holding onto my sanity during the times when I most needed it.

I still head out to the cabin for various reasons. Sometimes to read, to relax, listen to the radio or just to think. It has actually turned out to be a positive for me in so many ways. It's been an important location for respite, and still is a way of rejuvenating my spirits and a reflective way to recharge my batteries.

The difficult times are not easy to forget. But, there were also such wonderful and memorable times as well that I try to keep in the front of my memory. For instance, fishing with my kids are memories that I remember with great fondness. I'm not what you would call an avid fisherman. I can pretty much count on my toes, in one shoe, the number of fish I've caught in my entire life. But that didn't stop us from going with high expectations. We woke up early, packed the car and headed out when we were certain the fish would surely be biting. After a couple hours we came to the realization that the fish must not be hungry, and decided to call it quits. One time, Matthew and I purchased some fish at the local grocery store before going home. We put them in the pail and showed everyone all the fish we had caught. We had discarded all of the packaging, but since the fish were all cleaned and with no heads, we didn't fool anyone. It didn't really matter because we sure had a good laugh! We had many good times and those memories are precious.

You may have noticed that I've used the phrase 'deal with it.' That's what I do when faced with a problem. I identify it, then think about it, come up with a plan, good or otherwise and implement it the best way I can. This is the way I've always handled things. It's similar to working with tools in order to complete a task. I first identify the issue, make a plan, pick the right tools and go at it. This is what I mean by dealing with it. Maybe it's because I'm an engineer by trade, but that works for me. Dealing with a neurological situation, an area for which I had no training and little information, left me to figure it out the best way I could and then 'deal with it'. It became extremely frustrating when I knew that what I was doing wasn't working and no one could tell me what to do instead.

One of the most difficult times was when the rage episodes seemed to be coming one after another. We walked on eggshells hoping that the somewhat calm times would last a bit longer; but things always fell apart again. The constant breaking of furniture, kitchen chairs, windows and lamps was very difficult for me to experience. I whole-heartedly believed that one of my tasks as a father and husband was to keep things working and in good repair—that was my job. But these and other things were broken many times over. I know it was due to Matthew's symptoms but I couldn't help being frustrated and seeing it as an expression of his anger instead of symptoms. I really had such a hard time with that!

A difficult time was always when we tried to make Matthew go to his room to calm down after an episode of swearing, yelling and breaking furniture. He wouldn't go and we often had to carry him kicking, screaming and thrashing. Even this wasn't an answer because he destroyed whatever was in his room. It wasn't like this calmed him down; it didn't.

After one of these times that I was attempting to bring Matthew to his room and to his bed, his symptoms escalated to the point that he slapped me and spit in my face. I remember picking him up and dumping him onto the bed. I say *dumping,* but at that moment my actions were very close to being out-of-control. I heard his hand or arm hit the wall next to his bed with a loud thud. Suddenly I realized that I was dangerously close to losing control. It scared the hell out of me. Thoughts of my hurting him became so intense that I had to leave the room.

This could very easily have been considered abuse on my part. I felt ashamed. I felt like a bad father. I felt like a bad human being. I tried to convince myself that it was only an isolated expression of my anger. But it was more than that, and I was terrified that it might happen again. Losing control was scary for me. But if there is a positive, it was that I realized I needed to do something to get a grip because next time I might actually hurt him.

That whole episode made me face the realization that I had to make patience more meaningful and much more of a reality in the manner in which I responded to my son. I can't go back and change what had happened. I would if I could. But I think I learned from it. That incident forced me to realize that control can be a very thin line, and that line can be very fragile. It was one of those horrific yet valuable moments that made me a better parent.

These were painful times for everybody! I look back now and I thank God we made it through. I wish I knew precisely how we did it so I could share it with others going through similar situations. But I truly don't know how we all did it.

I am so very proud of my wife for her support and guidance when it was needed, and my kids because they grew up to be decent, hardworking adults who all love each other. I have a lot to be thankful for. I love my family very much. I am honored to be their husband and father.

- 19 -

Hello there! My Name is Matt.

I'd like to thank you for reading this book. I'm writing my chapter before reading any of the book myself, so I hope that whatever my Mom and Dad have written was helpful to you. I'm 30 years old now, and my life has been pretty incredible so far. Interesting for sure! Many difficult times but many awesome times too. I've been through a lot and want to share what I've experienced and learned along the way in my own words. I'd like to start by sharing with you my story so far.

First Grade

I was diagnosed with Tourette's when I was five years old. A year later, in first grade, a friend asked me why I was making some noises and twitches. I told him it was because I had Tourette's, which made me do these things that I couldn't help. His response was simply, "Oh, okay" and we went back to playing. His response shocked me. I was amazed how quickly and easily he understood and that it wasn't a big deal to him. Later that day, one of the kids in my class was making fun of me. My friend said, "Don't make fun of him. He can't help it because he has Tourette's." I was shocked again because he stood up for me. At that point I figured it would be a good idea to tell everyone in my class that I have Tourette's.

The next day I asked my teacher if I could tell all my classmates that I had Tourette's. She said yes and asked them all to sit on the floor. I sat on her lap in the rocking chair where she always sat when she read a story to us. She helped me tell them I had Tourette's and what it did to me. The bullying decreased and the understanding and acceptance increased for the rest of the year.

After that, I decided it would be a good idea to tell my classmates at the beginning of every school year that I had Tourette's. Within a few years everyone at my grade level knew about my condition. I had many friends and was well accepted in the normal school social life. All of the students knew that everyone else knew I had Tourette's, and the kids who might have teased me didn't because they knew they would have been hassled by the rest of our classmates.

SECOND GRADE

My second grade teacher was Mrs. Piraino, and all I can say is that she was an incredibly fantastic teacher! She helped me in so many ways. One of them was learning to use different techniques and strategies to help me get past some of my symptoms and be able to complete what I needed to get done.

I was given permission to be excused from the class if my symptoms were bad. I went to get a drink of water, or to another room where I let out a lot of my explosive tics and then returned to class. Mrs. Piraino and I developed a signal that I used while she was teaching that indicated I needed to leave.

When she asked me if I had any ideas as to what the signal should be, I said that I would raise my hand with two fingers up. At the time, I didn't realize it was a peace sign. I guess I was born to be a peaceful kind of guy (Ha ha ha). She responded by either gently shaking her head yes or no. If she was teaching something important and I really needed to be in class to hear it, she very gently shook her head no. But I was confident that as soon as it was okay for me to leave, she would nod her head yes and I would go. By doing this, it was much less of an interruption to the rest of the class than it would have been for me to ask out loud every time I needed to be excused. It was simple, quick, quiet, respectful and effective.

My symptoms were gradually getting worse and worse at that time. She made me feel like it was okay and that she was there to help me get through both my difficult symptoms and the school year. If I had a hurdle to jump, then she placed a stepladder in front of the hurdle to help me jump over it. That's how I felt as her student. I felt at ease because she never gave up on me and always had a way for me to get through my challenges so I could still learn and continue on to the third grade.

Creating a signal with Mrs. Piraino taught me that using strategies could be helpful. As I went on through school, I learned and developed other strategies to use in higher grades.

THIRD GRADE, RPC, EASTMAN SCHOOL OF MUSIC

At eight years old, my symptoms were so uncontrollable that I lived at Rochester Psychiatric Center (RPC) for a little over a year. The hardest part was being separated from my family and my friends.

I remember the day I went to live there. It was a very large, off-white building with front doors in the middle. The right half of the building had small windows, and the left side had a very tall fence with very mean-looking barbed wire circles wrapping around the top of it. The same kind of barbed wire fencing that was used for prisons. I found out that it actually was a prison on that side of the building—criminals who were classified as mentally insane were locked up there.

Thankfully I was living on the right side of the building. But to me it didn't matter. I was still forced to live there. It was a prison to me. I wasn't able to go outside unless I was instructed to do so by the staff. There were three heavy locked doors to get into the place I was living for the next year of my life...at eight years old. I wondered why I was there. Why was I being locked up for being born? I knew I got out of control at times, but I couldn't help it and never wanted to do so. It didn't make a lot of sense to me back then.

I told myself, "I will behave next time I see my family." I never acted up with anyone else. I could do it! I was always so happy to see my family, and I decided to show them I could behave so I could go home and be with them again. But when they visited me, my symptoms got out of control again. Then I felt terrible and had to go another week at RPC without seeing them (or anyone else outside of RPC), hoping that I could behave at next week's one-hour visit. I was only permitted an hour visit once a week. It was awful to wait that long to see my family.

While I was living there, it seemed like many of the staff members hated being there as much as me. They got paid enough to live by and with good benefits from the state. Many of them just didn't care. There were a few that did, but some of them were pretty mean and very scary. I never acted up the entire year I was there. But all of the other kids living there did. They were restrained, kicking and screaming. Some of them got a shot in the butt to calm down if they were getting way out of control. Many times I heard them cry while they were being restrained, saying that they couldn't breathe. The staff responded, "If you can't breathe then how are you talking?"

I was never restrained, but I once asked a staff member to put me in a restraint because I was curious to know what it felt like. She put me in a restraint, sitting up, which was what they did at times. It was a very gentle restraint compared to what I saw happen to the other kids, and I wasn't throwing a fit, so I knew it would have been much worse if it was real. It was painful and it really was difficult to breathe. I can't imagine what it must have felt like to actually be restrained. Especially when the kids were forced to lay down with heavy full-grown adults lying on top of them.

RPC was not a place I wanted to stay. All I wanted to do was to go home. I missed my family so much! My bedtime was at 8:30 p.m. My mom and I came up with the idea to look outside the window at exactly 8:30 to look at the moon and say goodnight to one another. It was a way for her and I to stay connected to each other.

Even though the rules said that I wasn't supposed to leave RPC for any reason, my mom was somehow able to convince the doctors that I should go back to the school I attended before I lived there. She also convinced them to allow one of my parents to pick me up every Saturday morning to take drum lessons from the lead percussionist of the Rochester Philharmonic Orchestra at The Eastman School of Music.

Both of these accomplishments were nothing short of a miracle! Somehow, Mom managed to get the attention of the people at RPC who were sensitive to my needs and convinced them to make the best decisions for my situation rather than focusing on the rules. I think my mom was very good at maneuvering her way around the not-so-understanding and not-so-flexible people. She was like a persistent breeze, respectfully getting things done that needed to be done with a calmness that didn't ruffle any feathers. She's always been good at that. I think a lot of it had to do with the way she would speak with honesty, compassion, determination, and logic. She's pretty incredible!

I loved taking percussion lessons at the Eastman School of Music and it was very important for me, especially while living at RPC. It was something that kept me going. Six days of every week felt like a dark thunderstorm at RPC, and every Saturday was the day of sunshine when I would take lessons at Eastman. I was able to continue learning what I loved to do from an amazing teacher, Ruth Cahn. She was an incredible percussionist, and an astonishing teacher and person!

As a little kid, I was so happy that Ruth was willing to provide me lessons every week. She was elegant, classy, strong yet gentle, with a huge heart and the utmost tolerance and patience. Any time I had to tic, she would wait until I was done and continued on with the lesson like nothing unusual had happened. Ruth never treated me as if I were different from anyone else. To her, I was an exceptional student and a young person to teach and inspire with percussion lessons. I always knew she believed in me and respected my abilities. It was if my Tourette syndrome didn't even exist to her. I continued taking lessons from her every week for the next eight years.

Another person who was important to my life was Mr. DeLoria. He was the principal of the school that I was allowed to attend in third grade while living at RPC. It was important for me to go back to my regular school. It was nice to see my friends that I had known since my preschool years even though I could never hang out with them after school. The school was for students in Kindergarten through third grade, and the school band started in fourth grade. By the third grade I was already a decent drummer after taking lessons from a couple high school drummers since Kindergarten and about a year of lessons from Ruth.

Mr. DeLoria was a bit of a musician himself, and we had many conversations about music. He would joke around with me that someday we would perform a rock concert in front of the entire school. At the end of third grade, he called me to the office and said, "Matthew, ask your parents to bring your drum set into school on Friday. We're going to have a huge rock concert for the whole school with my band and you as our drummer." I felt like I had just won the lottery!

My parents brought in my drum set and we had a concert with his band in front of all the kids and teachers. It was one of the most memorable moments in my life…even to this day. After the concert was over, all the students went back to our homerooms to get ready to go home or, in my case, to RPC. While I was in my homeroom still smiling ear to ear and floating on cloud nine, my teacher told me that there was a group of 'fans' that wanted my autograph. All of the third graders were lined up down the hall holding papers and pens. I signed as many as I could before the teachers told everyone it was time to go home.

I remember that day as being a great experience and high point in my life. Living at RPC was very difficult and I didn't have much fun in my life, except for drum lessons on Saturdays. Playing in my first rock concert showed me that life can be a good thing. It gave me a lot of hope, courage, strength, and confidence to keep pushing forward through the hard times I was dealing with, and the hard times that were still to come. It was nice seeing the respect and admiration from my classmates. Nothing on earth could have broken my spirits at that time.

I met Sheriff Meloni, a great man, when I was eight. He was my RPC Compeer, an adult who volunteers time to spend with kids and adults who need extra support. He was also the Sheriff of Monroe County for many years and was one of the most well respected people in Rochester. This became obvious every election year because no one would run against him knowing that he would win.

Sheriff Meloni helped kids at RPC by spending time with them, taking them out for pizza and fun activities. I remember one time that he brought me to his work and took me to the prison where the inmates were held. Since I was only eight years old at the time, I was pretty scared. I thought they would be similar to the people I saw on TV; I was afraid they were going to kill me.

When we first entered the jail, Sheriff Meloni was greeted with obvious respect by all of the officers. Of course, that made perfect sense because he was their boss. But inside the area where the inmates were housed, he got the same amount of respect from the prisoners. I'm not talking about the fake kind of respect that an authority figure gets based on fear. I'm talking about a genuine respect. I'll never forget what he told me, "These people are like everyone else but have made a mistake and have to do the time for it. That's all." It was his genuine and caring attitude of respect for all people that earned everyone's admiration. Sheriff Meloni was an inspiration for the people of Monroe County, the police officers and even the people who had been arrested.

Incredibly he was, and still is, my friend.

CRESTWOOD CHILDREN'S CENTER

After a year at RPC, I moved to another facility called Crestwood Children's Center. This was a huge improvement. As a little boy, I thought a lot of the staff that worked there were pretty cool. But I'd have to say I saw Jodi, a man who worked in the cottage where I lived, as being on the top of my "coolest" list. It didn't hurt that he was also a musician!

But there was more to Jodi than just being a cool guitar player. He was always supportive and helpful to me when I was having a particularly difficult time. He saw my difficulties as due to my symptoms instead of being a bad kid. The day I left, he walked me to the car to say goodbye. I truly believed then—and continue to believe—that he cared about me. It was more than just a job for him to watch over us kids. He really cared about us and saw us all as good kids that needed a little help. I lived at Crestwood for about a year, and then I lived at a foster home for two years after Crestwood.

Sixth Grade

In sixth grade, I had a chorus teacher named Mrs. Stewart. She worked with the entire class to put on a musical show. She told us that it would be performed in front of the entire school as well as a few evenings for family and friends. There were only a small handful of lead roles. I, of course, wanted one of the lead roles—as did the majority of the other 100-plus students in chorus. I was afraid Mrs. Stewart wouldn't consider me for one of the roles because of my symptoms.

When she chose me for one of the lead parts, I was thrilled beyond belief. When you think about it, it didn't make any sense to have me play a lead role; with all my symptoms to deal with, it very logically could have been a disaster. But she was one of those people who saw others without bias and acted from her heart. She gave me a chance and believed in me.

Granted, the role I played was a young boy who was a little hyper, so it was kind of a good fit, but the role also involved a lot of speaking parts and good acting. Another person might have been afraid to give me the role, or believed I didn't deserve it, or that I wasn't suited for such an important role. Mrs. Stewart believed in me and gave me the chance to shine and I did!

That year, I also decided to compete in the school talent show for the first time. I played a drum set solo that I composed. I was really hamming it up, the girls in the crowd were screaming and I was absolutely loving it! I won first place that year. The first, second, and third place winners went on to compete in the county talent show. I didn't even place in the county talent show that year.

Coming Home and Seventh to Ninth Grade

When I was in seventh grade, I was bullied by a group of eighth graders in gym class, and I didn't understand why. Sure, I could have thrown a couple punches at them. I was smaller than they were and probably wouldn't have won. But even if I did, it wouldn't have been the best way to get them to stop or to end the problem. It would have just escalated the situation, which could have led to all sorts of negative scenarios.

Instead, I told a teacher what was going on. That teacher made them stay after school for a week. They had to research, learn and write an essay about Tourette and why they should treat all people better. That lesson was so much better than a couple of cuts and bruises. It was effective and led to a positive outcome! The bullies felt bad for their actions. They never again acted that way towards me, and I know it wasn't because the teachers forced them to behave. They never acted that way again because they didn't want to treat me that way. That was good in many ways! They didn't pick on me after school when there were no teachers around, and I bet they didn't pick on anyone else with Tourette or other people with disorders. I actually became good friends with one of them. It turned out that the best way to deal with the bullies was the firm, positive, and compassionate way.

When I first started living at RPC, my parents told me that when the day came for me to move back home, they would have a limo take me there. Four years later, I finally walked out the door to see a limo parked in the street. My parents were standing next to it and my brother, cousin and best friend were inside the limo ready to take me home. When the limo pulled into my driveway, I saw a lot of friends, family and neighbors standing outside in the front yard welcoming me back. I can't describe to you the feeling of living back home. That was all I could think about every day for four years. It may not sound like much as an adult, but as a kid at that age, it's everything! That day was HUGE! I was home. I was HOME! I WAS HOME!!!

I was living at home with my family. My Mom! My Dad! My brother! My sister! I woke up in the morning and there they were! I ate dinner with them! I went to the movies with my friends. I went to my friends' houses and they came over to mine. I went to their birthday parties. I went to after-school programs and participated in the soccer and track teams. I played in the school band and in my own bands with friends. I had a normal life! I entered the local school talent show again in seventh grade and won first place even though I was competing against students in grades seven through twelve. I also competed in the county talent show, but I didn't place.

I also entered a music competition called the New York State School Music Association (NYSSMA) solo festival. At NYSSMA, students in New York state learn solos and perform them for a judge. If your score is high enough, you're asked to participate in an all-county and/or all-state music ensemble. The levels of solo difficulty range from 1-6, where 1 is the easiest and 6 is the hardest. I did a level 5 snare drum solo. It's pretty rare for a seventh grader to be able to perform a level 5. I earned a score of 100 points—a perfect score!

In both eighth and ninth grades, I performed level 6 solos and earned perfect scores on those, too. In eighth grade, I also played a drum set solo in the local school talent show and won second place. The first place winner was a band that rocked out pretty darn good to the song "Stairway to Heaven." Every year after that, up through my senior year, I won first place.

172

Sophomore, Junior, and Senior Years

My high school years were fun. From ninth through twelfth grades, I went to a private high school that had smaller class sizes. I was able to learn much better that way. I was still able to participate in my local school's activities and after-school programs. I did some acting in a few shows in high school drama classes. It was nice hanging out with friends, going on dates and having girlfriends, going to the junior and senior proms, graduating from high school and going off to college. I had a relatively normal high school life.

In high school, I needed to figure out a way to get copies of the notes in class because there was no way I could write my own. I found someone who took good notes and asked them to use a sheet of carbon paper (back in the day) so I could have a copy. Since my symptoms interfered with taking legible notes, I wouldn't have learned much because my entire focus would have been on attempting to catch up. By asking a classmate for a copy of the notes, I was able to focus and listen to the teacher a lot easier.

I also developed another strategy to release my extra energy so I could behave better in class. During study hall, I was permitted to run around the track a couple of times to burn off some steam and return before the next class started. If I wasn't allowed to do that, I would have caused a lot of trouble in that class. I couldn't do homework in the study hall because my Attention Deficit Disorder (ADD) at the time was too extreme to allow me to work silently for an entire class period. It made sense to use that time in a productive manner to run around the track.

I continued entering talent shows during my high school years. At the county level, I won third place during my sophomore year, first place in my junior year, and third place again as a senior. The summer between sophomore and junior year, I entered the county fair talent show. I was kind of full of myself when it came to my drumming skills and thought I didn't need to practice. I figured since I win them all anyways, I'll win this one too. I was humbled with a 32nd place. I entered that talent show again the following year, and practiced a lot, and I won first place. From there, I went to the next round a week later at the state fair talent show, and I did pretty good. Then I was selected to continue on to the semi-finals the following week. But that was as far as I got.

COLLEGE AND BEYOND

I went to college for a year and realized I was majoring in something I didn't want to do for a career. I took some time off to figure that out. During that time, I was employed at an arts center that worked with people who had disabilities, adolescents who were at-risk, and other adults and kids from the community. This arts center provided classes in music, visual arts, dance and theater. I realized how much I enjoyed working with people and helping them through the arts.

I considered going back to college for human services, but wasn't sure which area was a good fit for me. While I was trying to figure that out, a service coordinator who I used to work with mailed me an article about drum circles. I was instantly interested in checking them out. So I started doing research, and attended a few drum circles. Then I facilitated my first drum circle! That was the moment I felt awakened to what I wanted to do for a living.

I received a grant to start my company, called Drum Echoes, Inc., that provides drumming services. Through my business, I can now help others in the same way my drumming has helped me throughout my life! I run drumming programs for people of all ages, backgrounds and abilities. One of my drumming programs is facilitating drum circles. It can be a fun way to have a physical, mental and emotional outlet. It's also a great way to learn and play the drums by playing together with a group.

I also write and direct percussion ensembles and theater productions. Being in theater production was a good thing for me growing up because it taught me the discipline to work hard by practicing my drumming or acting roles. It's a great way to work with others and learn to get along with them by working towards the same overall purpose—to put on a great performance. When that happens, it brings a great feeling of accomplishment as a team.

Using what I have learned in my life, I give inspirational presentations and teambuilding workshops. I use the drums as a tool for teaching while making it fun for the audience. They get to drum while learning. I enjoy providing these drumming workshops for schools, colleges, camps, health care facilities, conferences, corporations, private events and anywhere else there is a group of people who can benefit from my services.

Audiences and participants describe their experience as not only entertaining, inspiring, and educational, but as also helping their physical, mental and emotional well-being. I can't begin to describe the joy I feel knowing that I've helped renew their enthusiasm and excitement for life. I love this work! In case you're interested, my website is www.drumechoes.com.

On July 4, 2010, I moved to Denver, Colorado to chase my dream. I didn't have any work lined up, knew only one person who lived here and had only enough money to get me by for three months. I knew little about the state. All I really knew about it was that it had the Rocky Mountains, a city called Denver and an amazing performing arts center where many Broadway shows get their beginnings. While continuing to provide drumming services, I want to reach for something more with my career. I love the theater. My next goal is creating a Broadway show. As I write this chapter, it's been two years since the move. I've made some amazing friends, and have some incredible stories and experiences I can tell my grandkids someday.

I've also made some great connections with people in the theater business to make this Broadway show a reality. I don't know when it will happen. But my love, hard work and passion for this are so great, it *will* happen! My goals in life are many. I want to light up Broadway in NYC and throughout the world. Get married and have a wonderful family. Continue with my drumming work. Live an eventful, satisfying and purposeful life. When I'm old and grey, I want to be able to think to myself that I did a good job in my life. I want to know I did well for myself and made a positive difference for others. I think I'm doing pretty good so far, and I'm excited to hopefully have a lot more to go!

- 20 -

VALUABLE LIFE LESSONS

My parents were always there for me and helped me a lot. I recognize how much they helped me by not helping me at times too. As a result, I learned to live, survive and succeed in the real world. I knew they were there for me, but I also knew that I had to learn how to walk in this life on my own. They taught me that when I fall down, I have to pick myself back up and continue walking. I knew I had to do this if I wanted to someday live as a successful and independent person.

Learning how to stand on my own two feet has been important for me, but it sure does help to have supportive, loving people in my life to help me get through it. We are all individuals, but we are individuals living in this world together. We all need love and support from others to survive. As independent as you may be, you have to admit that. Even all by yourself in the wilderness, living off the land, you still need others. They might be other plants and animals, but you still need them and they need you.

That give-and-take relationship in a balanced community was something I strongly needed as a child to survive. Now that I have grown past those difficult times, I've gained a greater understanding of the need for that balanced community throughout all forms of life. Nothing in this world can survive entirely on its own. We need to be there for each other and not just ourselves. Living as a community is important and a really beautiful thing!

I think we all pretty much want the same things from life: success, friends, living independently, relationships, love, good health, piece of mind, freedom and happiness. This can sometimes be harder to achieve for people who have neurological disorders. We can easily fall victim to the attitude that these things will never happen for us because of the many disappointments we have experienced in the past.

I have to take a lot more hits in life than most people. That's my life. But it doesn't mean I can't achieve the things in life that I want. In some ways, my Tourette's has taught me many skills that I can use to achieve those things better and quicker than others. I can take a hit and know how to keep pushing forward. I've gained a greater understanding how to approach life and people in a caring, understanding and compassionate way, which can help with relationships. In many ways, my Tourette's has helped me a great deal to become an even better and more successful person in life than if I didn't have Tourette's.

A MESSAGE FOR ADULTS

My Mom and Dad are great! But they're not perfect. As great as they have been throughout my life, they made some wrong choices and they can drive me nuts at times. But I still love them and I know they love me. I am very, very grateful to be their son.

You're not expected to be perfect parents or adults and you're not going to be. Life doesn't work that way. The journey of life is not designed for us to be perfect. It's designed for us to do the best we can and to learn from the experiences life gives us and by the choices we make. Do the best you can as a parent, teacher, friend, relative, etc. Please don't beat yourself up too much if you don't do everything perfectly.

I'm not saying that you shouldn't care. Caring is a very good thing, so please continue to care. But it's normal—and can be a good thing—to feel guilty from making mistakes. Guilt makes us learn from it by either fixing our mistakes or by making better choices next time. I'm just saying it's not good to hold onto guilt for too long. Please have some compassion and understanding for yourself. I see my parents and other parents beat themselves up way too much over something so silly.

I'm saying this to my parents right now, too. Let it go! I love you, Mom and Dad, and you know I'm doing great! I'm not mad or disappointed for anything you've ever done. I'm only happy and grateful for all that you both are and for being the most wonderful, loving and supportive parents to me. To all parents out there, I can only imagine how hard yet rewarding it is to be a parent. I know that being a parent of a child with challenging behaviors is difficult. You're dealing with situations where there are no definite answers. It's not black and white, and some things work for one family and other things work better for another.

If you are reading this book you obviously care, so you are already doing something right. Just keep loving your kids, caring for them, and doing what you can to help them out and to get them through their challenges. Please know that success is a reality that can be achieved no matter how difficult dealing with challenging behaviors may currently be.

Another piece of very important advice is to take time to care for yourself. You deserve it and need it. Your kids need you to take care of yourself too. The healthier you are, the better you can help out and take care of your kids. It's a selfish thing that we all need to do at times, but it's also a selfless thing too. Please take care of yourself!

FREEDOM TO BE NORMAL

Every kid desires to live a normal and successful life with other people who are living 'normal' lives. I think it's really important that all kids have opportunities to socialize and participate in activities with other kids even if it's difficult. They may even learn better social skills by making socially inappropriate mistakes. Try to keep kids socializing with their peers as much as possible. Even more so with activities they are good at or have a passion for. It gives them a common ground with their peers that can help them to socialize without their disorder being a main focus.

One of the greatest things my parents taught me was to never feel ashamed of having Tourette's. They used to tell me all the time when I was young that I'm a normal and charming 11 year old kid who has brown hair, hazel eyes, and Tourette's; is 4 feet 11 inches tall and weighs 95 pounds. Tourette's is a small part of who I am, not the only part. I can't help what I'm doing because this is how I was born and there is nothing wrong with that. You wouldn't tell a blind man to just work harder at seeing; it would only frustrate him and make him feel worse.

Diversity is a beautiful thing, even with people. Everyone is different and we should embrace and appreciate that. Thank God we are all different! I think I'm a pretty awesome guy, but I certainly would not want this world to be populated with over 7 billion Matt Giordanos. We all deserve respect and to be treated equally, like everyone else, hands down! This is not debatable and not questionable! No one deserves to be mistreated for being born the way they are!

One of my approaches to educate others is having business cards that I keep in my wallet which state that I have Tourette syndrome. The card has a brief description of what it is and includes the Tourette Syndrome Association's website in case anyone wants to learn more about it. I never apologize for who I am, so that's not what the card is for. The card is just meant to educate people about my Tourette's. I hand the card out to people around me before a problem may arise, or when they're acting in ways they shouldn't towards me. For example, I hand them out to everyone sitting near me on an airplane as soon as I sit down. I also give one to the flight attendant as I board the plane. It's quiet, quick, easy and effective

I think it's important to keep a respectful compassion towards others while educating them. I try to remember that they simply may not know. People are generally good, so we need to treat them that way.

Expressing Feelings and Thoughts

One thing that has been extraordinarily helpful for me was being able to express my thoughts and feelings from an early age. Having the opportunity to see good therapists was a really positive thing for me. Talking openly and honestly with the people that are significant in my life is important too.

Dealing with Rage

When I was a kid having such extreme rage episodes, it was a scary thing for everyone, including me. I remember that I didn't have control of these rage episodes any more than I had control over my tics or OCD episodes. I just couldn't stop myself. When the rage finally calmed down, I felt like the worst person on the planet. I couldn't believe that I treated the people I loved the most in such a terrible way.

I always felt responsible, even though I wasn't. Intellectually, I knew it was the Tourette's, but the guilt was still overwhelming. After I had lost control and hurt the ones I loved, it wasn't as if I looked at myself in the mirror and thought, "It's the Tourette's fault. No big deal." I always believed that it was my fault. I blamed myself even though I knew it was my symptoms' fault and I had no control over any of these behaviors. It didn't matter though. I was the one who hurt the people I love, and I was the one who always felt so terrible about it.

As an adult, I don't have rage episodes anymore. I'm also able to recognize what triggers a lot of my symptoms. The environment can make my symptoms either worse or better. The air quality is important. If it has high levels of dust, molds, chemicals and other allergens, it can make my symptoms worse. If it's clean of them, my symptoms feel better. I've noticed electromagnetic signals from cell phones and wi-fi in my environment can increase my symptoms. Cell phone towers or being in a room with a lot of electrical appliances can make my symptoms worse, including increased frustration, irritability and anxiety. Other things that make a strong impact on my symptoms are sleep quality, exercise, nutrition and stress management.

I'm not a fan of medications. Some people have found success managing symptoms in more natural ways. Please take a look at these websites. Trust me, they are worth the look. They discuss many other environmental factors that can impact symptoms for many neurological disorders: www.ticsandtourettes.com and www.latitudes.org. I assure you that I receive no gains or benefits in any way from including this information, other than the honor of providing these resources to you.

IMPORTANCE OF DRUMMING

Drumming makes my symptoms go away. I don't know why or how but it does. I don't have tics when I drum. Drumming is also a great way to express myself emotionally and is a great way to let out all of my energy so I can relax a little better after I'm done. Another bonus is it helps people to look past my Tourette's. They usually see and treat me with respect and as an equal. Drumming has helped my confidence. It's made me feel I can do something well and accomplish anything if I work at it. It's helped me socially and to be able to work and get along with others. The drums have helped me in so many ways. It's good to play and practice by myself but it's also a good thing to play with other musicians I enjoy playing with.

Drumming was such a positive thing in my life. Drummers need to be able to play in a controlled manner that is soft, loud, slow and fast. That's a good form of control for people with Tourette's to develop. I typically like to start out by stretching and shaking my body off and then just letting it loose by playing the drums really fast and loud to let out my Tourette energy. It then allows me to play with better control, technique and dynamics without the interference of my Tourette symptoms. I can then work on strengthening my drumming skills that will then help the part of my brain that controls my motor skills and mental focus. I truly believe this is a very effective way to reduce my Tourette's symptoms.

I also encourage drummers to learn to read sheet music. Reading sheet music requires a greater level of mental focus and motor control. It also improves a drummer's ability to play and understand music a lot better. I'm just speaking from my own personal observation. I don't know if this is scientifically proven or not, but it is what I feel when I drum.

Overall, playing the drums has helped decrease my symptoms. When I feel stress or when my symptoms are more intense, I might take out my buffalo drum. By playing that drum, I feel myself calm down. I encourage youngsters and adults everywhere to try this any time they need to let energy out and want to relax. The buffalo drum has a beautiful and calming sound that resonates throughout the room really well. They may want to play the drum laying down, sitting down or standing up, dancing or stomping on the ground. They may want to sing or let out some vocal tics while playing. Offer the options, but leave it up to the individual to choose what to do.

In my experience, my Tourette's actually has given me an advantage that helps me be a better drummer. I believe that having Tourette increases my ability to drum, while my obsessive compulsive tendencies require a certain perfectionism that makes me keep practicing until I get it right. Tourette's and my drumming work in harmony, which negates the disability. Drumming helps reduce my Tourette's and my Tourette's helps me to become a better drummer. That's a pretty sweet deal if you ask me.

I strongly suggest that adults encourage their children to pursue whatever interest they may be passionate about besides watching TV and playing video games. They may be interested in music, dance, art, sports, science, theater, whatever; I believe that other passions and hobbies can bring the same gifts to people that drumming has brought to me.

PERSONAL REFLECTIONS

If I had a chance to change anything in my life, would I do it?...I don't know. I do know there are some things I wish I had said and done differently to my family and friends. I wish I was kinder, and had been more patient and understanding towards them at times. Sometimes I didn't stand up for what I knew was right and I wish I had. I wish I worked harder on certain things and not taken other things so seriously and gotten so worked up over them. But I guess that's all a part of life. Live and learn. Every moment of my life has made me who I am today, and is the reason why I am at the place I'm at today. I am thankful for all of it. So maybe I wouldn't change anything.

Life has its ways of throwing us around both pleasantly and unpleasantly. Our reactions to it and the way we throw ourselves back into it set our path. I know life isn't always fair and isn't always sunshine and roses. But even the roses need clouds to cover the sun and bring the rain, because the rain is needed as much as the warmth of the sun for the roses to grow. Sometimes the cold and dark moments are the greatest gifts. They can teach us and help to show us who we are and get to know our strengths. But we all need love and warmth from friends and family. Please allow yourself to receive it and allow yourself to give it. I've certainly needed the warmth and love from my family and friends to get through life. My knowledge and my heart have grown from all of my life's experiences that I was lucky enough to have.

I hope that sharing my family's experiences helps you on your journey. I hope they inspire you. I hope they give you some guidance, some courage and some peace of mind that everything can and will most likely be okay, and even great. I wish you the best as you and everyone in your life grow from all the experiences you have with each other. I wish you all the best as you all gain a greater knowledge and a stronger love as your life unfolds on its amazing and interesting journey. All of the experiences you and the people in your life have together are blessings!

Thank you for reading this book and for allowing my family to share with you our interesting and amazing journey.

- 21 -

REFLECTIONS OF A PROUD MOM

Dr. Oliver Sacks (the doctor that the movie "Awakenings" was based on) attended a drum circle in New York City facilitated by Matt. In 2007, Dr. Sacks wrote about this experience in his book, *Musicophilia*, which was on the *New York Times* Top Ten List for many weeks. The following is an excerpt from this book:

> "In New York City recently, I took part in a drum circle organized by Matt Giordano, a gifted drummer with severe Tourette's.....I could see eruptions of tics, contagions of tics, rippling around the thirty-odd Touretters there—but once the drum circle started, with Matt leading them, all the ticking disappeared within seconds. Suddenly there was synchronization, and they came together as a group, performing 'in the moment with the rhythm,' as Matt puts it—their Tourettic energy, motor exuberance, playfulness, and inventiveness all drawn upon creatively and given expression in the music. Music here had a double power; first, to reconfigure brain activity, and bring calm and focus to people who were sometimes distracted or preoccupied by incessant tics and impulses; and second, to promote a musical and social bonding with others, so that what began as a miscellany of isolated, often distressed or self-conscious individuals almost instantly became a cohesive group with a single aim—a veritable drum orchestra under Matt's baton."

That's *my* son he is talking about! Incredible! I wouldn't have guessed 15 years prior to this that an internationally respected author and doctor would be writing such a positive commentary about my little boy!

Matthew's resiliency and optimism have always amazed me. It was incredible that a child with so many difficulties was able to be such a happy kid and grow up to have such a positive outlook on life. There certainly have been times when sadness has blanketed his light. But, somehow he continues to toss aside that blanket and reveal to the world an optimistic and confident person with a hunger, recognition and respect for the beauty that life offers. One of his favorite songs, which he sometimes sings on my voice mail, is "Beautiful World." Matt does an amazing imitation of Louis Armstrong! It gives me a huge lump in my throat just thinking about it.

His dynamic personality has been such a blessing not only for him but also for the majority of people who have gotten to know him. His life has been filled with people who have been more than willing to go out of their way to help this little boy, teenager and young adult. I don't think I have ever spoken to a person who has touched Matt's life in some way who doesn't smile when they, or I, mention his name. It was in elementary school when I became aware that adults wanted to be part of his success story and his life. I saw the pride on their faces during many of his concerts as a youngster. I continue to see a similar expression when we talk about his accomplishments as an adult.

His positive attitude toward life is contagious. You only have to experience one of his drum circles or keynote presentations to be pulled into the power of his passion for life. His accomplishments as an adult are many:

Matt moved to Denver on July 4, 2010. Soon after this, the Canadian Tourette Syndrome Foundation sponsored a young filmmaker to produce a short documentary about Tourette syndrome for their webpage, @Random. This filmmaker, John Cullen, was interested in filming a musician and chose Matt.

During the filming, Matt made the comment, "I feel like a 75 watt light bulb plugged into a 1,000 watt socket." Thus the title of this 13 minute documentary—"75 Watts," which premiered at the Hot Docs Film Festival in Toronto, Canada in 2011. It won first place for Best Documentary Short at the 2011 Palm Spring International Film Festival. At the 2012 Academy of Canadian Cinema Awards, also held in Toronto, "75 Watts" was nominated for Best Short Documentary.

In 2008, Alan Yentob, Creative Director for the British Broadcasting Corporation (BBC) and a camera crew flew from Europe to spend two days filming and interviewing Matt. They even made the trek down dirt roads to our home in Conesus to see where he was brought up and to interview Tony and me. As a result, Matt was featured in both a BBC documentary, "Imagine...Oliver Sacks, Tales of Music and the Brain" and a Public Broadcasting Service (PBS) NOVA documentary, "Musical Minds."

A few weeks after Matt had facilitated a drum circle at a residential setting where adults with disabilities lived, one of the social workers that works there told Matt, "Not once has anyone ever seen Howard—a man who has lived in this residence for over 12 years—smile. When he participated in the drum circle, he smiled! Not a little grin, but a real, honest to goodness, smile."

John Raffaele, President Mid-Hudson Coalition for The Development of Direct Support Practice and Director of Staff Training and Development, New Hope Community, Loch Sheldrake, NY has asked Matt more than once to be a keynote at his agency. He wrote:

> "Matt Giordano is 'The Ramones' of keynote speakers. The punk rock band The Ramones would start their concerts with an explosion and end with a louder one, and in the middle was a constant barrage of sound, emotion and power. Matt does this in the context of the subject matter he presents during his keynote. His personal story and testimony are moving and very powerful. That in itself is impactful but his

drumming...well, his drumming will electrify and motivate audiences of all ages and backgrounds. Being in a room of 400 people, all of whom are directed by Matt's incredible facilitation, was one of the most powerful and spiritual moments I have ever had at a keynote presentation.

The most important part of my recommendation of Matt is as follows: he helps people understand that disability is a social construction. Disability does not matter ultimately in people's lives just as long as they have the right support, information and love. Knowing Matt, I do not see disability. I see an amazing drummer and a person and speaker that will help you understand the uselessness of diagnosis and the usefulness of seeing people first!"

There were people who told me when Matt was young that his aggressive behaviors would "generalize" and he would most likely need to live in a residential placement as an adult. I knew my son; I never believed that for an instant! Anyone who knows Matt now is stunned at the thought of that possibility.

As I write this, I wonder about the physical phenomenon that makes a person's chest feel like it's going to burst whenever they feel pride. I don't know *how* it happens, but it is precisely what I feel every time I think about Matt, and how incredibly proud I am of the man that he has become.

Matt *is* that complex and beautiful mobile my friend said described him so many years ago. He is multi-talented, charming, and handsome. He can be funny as well as insightful. Discussions with Matt often leave me considering aspects of life as I never have before. He has an energy from deep inside him that he shares with the world. If you want to know what Matt is like, ask someone who has participated in one of his drum circles, seen him play music, heard him present at a conference or has known him on a personal level. For a glimpse of Matt today, watch "75 Watts" on his website, www.drumechoes.com

I'm not suggesting that everything is a bed of roses for Matt now that he is an adult. He continues to have symptoms that cause him more grief than a mother would want for her son. But he also continues to have that same optimism and joy for life he has had since a youngster.

I'll end with one last anecdote. One recent Sunday morning my good friend and minister, Rev. Dr. Deborah Roof, provided the congregation with two pieces of paper. On one, we were to write something we see as being a difficulty that we would like to turn over to God. On the other, she encouraged us to write something we see as being a blessing. On the blessing paper I wrote the following:

A major blessing in my life for which I am grateful is my son, Matt, being born with severe Tourette syndrome. While no mother would wish so many struggles for her son, I cannot ignore the many life lessons I have learned because of Matt. Because of him, I have been fortunate enough to have co-workers for whom I have the greatest respect and have learned so much. I also have had the pleasure of working with incredible families who have inspired me while teaching me much about life and parenting. Because of Matt, my life has been one of purpose, value, and incredible growth.

Every day I thank God for my incredible family, the love that we share and our interesting journey together.

Final Thoughts

During the process of writing this book, it became increasingly evident to me that we were extremely fortunate to have so many remarkable, talented and kind people who made such a positive contribution to our lives. Influential people, famous people and people who, because of their innate kindness, aided us on our quest: Dr. Oliver Sacks, Sheriff Meloni, Ruth Cahn, Matt's teachers, therapists, doctors, friends, family, and even strangers.

I owe a great deal of gratitude to the families who remind me daily how important it is to let parents know that having a child with challenging behaviors isn't their fault or the fault of their child—*and* that they are *not* alone. My sincere wish is that parents recognize and encourage your child's talents and interests, disregarding what anyone else thinks or says. Also, no matter how difficult, it is important that you *try* not to take symptoms personally and instead help your child discover ways to manage his or her difficulties. Love them even when it's hard to *like* them. And know it's very likely that someday you will look back at these times as being the hard years that are long past.

I am grateful for the critically important contributions of the people who volunteered to read numerous drafts of this book. This is especially true of four people. Liz Greenberg: without her subtle—and not-so-subtle—nudging, this book that I have talked about writing since Matt was a young boy would most likely never have been written. My co-workers, Jackie Yingling and Roger Nellist spent invaluable hours before work, during lunch, and even during their vacations, looking over each page with me. Jennifer Rowe provided us the exceedingly important professional and technical help we needed to finally get this to the publisher.

I thank my co-workers who read my original draft and met with me over pizza to discuss their thoughts and suggestions. Their encouragement and continuous reminders that there are families—as well as professionals—dealing with a wide variety of difficulties and diagnoses who would benefit from our story kept me moving forward. Thanks, Laura Arrington, April Dixon, Colleen Brown, Julie Buick, Linda Chadderdon, Cheri Greenauer, Cindy Hempel, Noranne Shiner, and Carrie Burkin. I am hopeful that in some small way, I have been of assistance on your journeys.

Resources

Neither the authors nor the publisher receive compensation for providing these resources. Website addresses may change.

"75 Watts" documentary
www.drumechoes.com/press.html

Association for Comprehensive Neurotherapy
www.latitudes.org

Autism Speaks
http://www.autismspeaks.org

Carol Gray
www.thegraycenter.org/social-stories

Carol Kranowitz
www.out-of-sync-child.com/articlesinterviews

Children and Adults with Attention Deficit Disorder
www.chadd.org

Dr. Oliver Sacks
www.oliversacks.com

Dr. Ross Greene
www.livesinthebalance.org

Drum Echoes, Inc.
www.drumechoes.com
International Obsessive Compulsive Disorder Foundation
www.ocfoundation.org

John Cullen
www.commarts.com/fresh/john-cullen.html

Kathie Snow: Disability is Natural
www.disabilityisnatural.com

Learning Disability Association
www.ldanatl.org

National Center for Learning Disabilities
www.ncld.org

Natural Treatments for Tics & Tourette's
www.ticsandtourettes.com

PACER Center
www.pacer.org

Rick Lavoie
www.ricklavoie.com

The Advocacy Center
www.advocacycenter.com

Tourette Foundation of Canada
www.atrandom.ca

Tourette Syndrome Association, Inc.
www.tsa-usa.org

Upstate NY Families for Effective Autism Treatment
www.usnyfeat.org

Wrights Law Special Education Law and Advocacy
www.wrightslaw.com

About The Authors

Matt Giordano is the owner and President of Drum Echoes, Inc., which he founded in 2003 to share his passion for percussion by facilitating drum circles and directing theater productions. Matt has been featured in numerous printed articles, interviews, television shows and the award-winning short documentary, "75 Watts." As a keynote presenter, he inspires international audiences to understand and celebrate their own and children's unique abilities.

Kathy Giordano has been a voice for parents of children with challenging and misunderstood behaviors for over 20 years. As a nationally recognized presenter, she educates school personnel, human service agencies and parent groups on the complexities of neurological disorders with behavior issues. She advocates the use of positive and proactive supports—instead of punishments that often increase negative behaviors—for children with these issues.

In *A Family's Quest for Rhythm*, Kathy writes candidly about keeping her family intact while raising her own son with behaviors and discovering the strategies that allowed him to become a successful adult. Kathy is currently an education advocate at The Advocacy Center and the Education Specialist for the National Tourette Syndrome Association, Inc.